Crockery Pot Cooking

Theodora FitzGibbon was born of Irish parents in London and educated in London and Europe. A doyenne of culinary art, her previous books on cooking include *Eat Well and Live Longer*, *The Art of British Cooking* and *The Food of the Western World* as well as the famous 'Taste of . . .' series of which Paris is the sixth.

Previously published by
Theodora FitzGibbon in Pan Books

A Taste of Ireland
A Taste of Scotland
A Taste of Wales
A Taste of England: The West Country
A Taste of London
A Taste of Paris

Theodora FitzGibbon

Crockery Pot Cooking

Pan Books London and Sydney

First published 1978 by Pan Books Ltd,
Cavaye Place, London SW10 9PG
© Theodora FitzGibbon 1978
ISBN 0 330 25518 5
Printed and bound in Great Britain by
Cox & Wyman Ltd, London, Reading and Fakenham

Acknowledgements
My thanks are due to Mrs Carol McCartney, Director of
the Good Housekeeping Institute, Miss Mary McFadyen
of Forbes Publications, Mrs Dianne Page of Tower
Housewares and my friend Maggie Black, all of whom
have been most helpful and given me valuable information
for this book.

Contents

Introduction 7

How to Use and Care for Your Slow Cooker 9

Soups and Soup-stews 11

Fish 21

Poultry and Game 32

Meat 62

Sauces 103

Vegetables 109

Sweet Dishes 117

Tea Breads and Cakes 129

Miscellaneous (Chutneys, Preserves, Jams
Beverages and Punch) 133

Index 139

For Jacqueline

with affection and gratitude
for all the encouragement over the years

Introduction

There is nothing new in the slow-cooking method; it has been known for centuries that long, slow cooking not only tenderized food but also brought out all the flavours. The simmering cauldron, the haybox, the fuel-burning range produced excellent food but with a lot of watching and extra work for the cook.

What is new is that similar results can now be produced in your home, without the watching and the work, by a small and attractive-looking electric crockery pot, which also gives the extra bonus of retaining many vitamins that could be destroyed by higher temperatures.

Basically they are thick stoneware casseroles set in a casing that contains a low-powered heating element, wound either around the sides, or in the case of some crockery pots which can be lifted out, on the bottom. The food is therefore evenly surrounded by heat and there is no fear of sticking or burning.

There are two temperature settings* – LOW and HIGH – which means you can leave it on all day, or night, without worry, in much the same way as you do a refrigerator. On the LOW setting liquid won't boil and the water condensation from the lid not only bastes the food and keeps it moist but also provides a liquid seal around the lid so that there is no evaporation and the food does not shrink in cooking.

The cost at LOW is roughly the same as running a 60–70 watt electric lightbulb, and at HIGH between 120–170 watts, depending on which cooker you choose. Therefore not only is the food cooked to

* These temperature settings apply to the crockery pots at present on sale in the United Kingdom and Ireland. In Europe there is the NOVA 2000 which has four settings, 1 to 10 and the wattage is 300. Therefore the heat control has a larger range, but all the recipes in this book can be used with this cooker, providing the instructions given in the accompanying Nova booklet are followed.

advantage, but there is a considerable saving in fuel which soon pays for the cost of the slow cooker. To cook a beef stew in an oven takes about 1.16 units of electricity; an electric ring about .84 and a slow cooker .65 units. Overnight it is even cheaper.

However, apart from the fuel saving, the crockery pot has the marvellous advantage that once the food has been prepared and put in, it is *better* not looked at at all. Peeping only lowers the temperature, which can take between 20 and 30 minutes to build up again. Another advantage is that the crockery pot is attractive enough to serve from at the table.

Obviously it has great advantages for people who are out at work all day or even part of the day. Not only can your lunch or dinner be waiting for you when you get home, but there is no odious cooking smell, just a most mouth-watering aroma to greet you. It is also useful for cooking large quantities and then freezing them. It is also an essential piece of kitchen equipment for the elderly. People with old and stiff joints find it difficult to bend down to ovens and lift out heavy and hot pots, then carry them to the table. With the crockery pot which can be plugged in and put on a table, all preparation of fish, poultry, meat or vegetables can be done at that table while sitting down, and then, when it is cooked, served from the same place. In cases of illness, nourishing soups or casseroles can be plugged in beside the bed, thus saving many trips up and down stairs, perhaps.

Questions have been raised as to whether the heat in the slow cooker is high enough to kill off bacteria effectively, and the conclusions are most satisfactory, providing the instructions given with each recipe are followed. Briefly, they are that the cooker should be preheated on HIGH and also that the cooking time should not be shortened in the case of poultry or meats. Leftover food should not be left in the cooker, but cooled quickly and put into the refrigerator, and *never* put raw food into the cooker and leave it until you want to cook it, always keep the food in a cold place until cooking time.

With a little practice you will find the slow crockery pot cooker a real friend in the kitchen and wonder how you managed all the years without one.

Theodora FitzGibbon,
Dalkey, Co Dublin, Ireland, 1978

How to Use and Care for Your Slow Cooker

1 All the slow crockery pot cookers vary slightly in performance so it is *important* that you read the instruction and recipe booklet given with your cooker. This particularly applies to cooking times. Study a similar recipe and adapt the cooking time accordingly. Everyone's taste is not the same with regard to food, so become familiar with your cooker before you experiment too much. After that you can put your imagination into play, but do not cut down drastically on cooking times of meat and poultry.

2 See that all frozen foods are properly thawed out before cooking. The heat is not enough to defrost and kill organisms, so think a little ahead and take foods from the freezer in good time.

3 Fats do not reduce in the crockery pot, so either trim off fat, or brown first and drain fat off before putting into the cooker. Or stand on a trivet and drain fat off before serving. If the meat is lean then there is no need to brown first; it is a matter of personal taste.

4 Voltage drops can affect the crockery pot and this is often reflected in the room lights and sometimes the television. If voltage seems very low, then check that the food is cooking normally, otherwise either lengthen cooking time or turn to HIGH if cooking on LOW. See also **5**.

5 If you want to hasten cooking put a sheet of foil over the food and under the lid, so that the heat is reflected back. This is a useful tip when the voltage is low.

6 When the cooker is required for only one or two people, put the ingredients into a smaller casserole which fits easily into the cooker, seeing that the lid sits easily, then pour boiling water to half-way up, cover and cook for 1 hour, approximately, less than the stated time.

7 Cool leftover food quickly, and place in another container before putting into the refrigerator. Make certain to bring it to boiling point before re-serving, unless it is something like a ham or tongue which is to be eaten cold.

8 Keep your cooker on a level surface where it will be safe from accidents, and avoid trailing flex, or flex touching the cooker.

9 Cooking at over 4,000 feet takes almost double the time owing to the lower atmospheric pressure at high altitudes.

10 Stir well before serving a casserole-type dish, so that all the flavours amalgamate thoroughly.

11 Crockery pot cookers in which the ceramic is not removable *must not* be immersed in water for cleaning. All cookers should be filled with hot soapy water and cleaned with a soft brush or cloth, not abrasive pads.

12 Do not put the crockery pot into the refrigerator with or without food inside it: in fact, do not use it as a storage container at all.

13 Apart from the recipes in this book and the booklet sold with it, the crockery pot can be used for heating up bread rolls, garlic bread, etc.

14 Plan your menus to give yourself the least amount of work. Take care of your crockery pot cooker, and it will take care of you.

15 *Do not peep during cooking*!

Soups and Soup-stews

To make a really good soup, stock is very important and it is easily made in a slow cooker. The bones can be left simmering all day or night and the liquid does not evaporate. Also, the slow cooking gives the flavours time to develop and merge together so that the maximum in taste is obtained. The stock can be frozen if not wanted for immediate use and it is better to freeze it in $\frac{1}{2}$ litre (1 pint) quantities so that practical amounts are available for casserole dishes, sauces and so on.

Almost any of your favourite soup recipes can be made in the crockery pot cooker, and I have tried to avoid those given in the booklet which comes with your cooker. Cooking methods vary slightly with the different cookers, so check your booklet before starting.

Some of these soups are very good for a simple buffet party, as they will keep hot without spoiling if the cooker is left at LOW. Served with crusty, hot garlic, or paprika bread (made by mixing paprika powder into the butter, then putting between the slices and wrapping in foil before reheating as for garlic bread), a selection of assorted cheeses, fruit and wine, it is almost party fare in itself. Or you have your first course all ready and hot, while you concentrate on the main dish.

There are some general rules for stock- and soup-making which should be read before beginning.

Rules for Soup-making

1 Preheat the cooker on HIGH for 20–30 minutes.

2 Do not use too many strong root vegetables such as onion, celery, turnip and parsnip as the long, slow cooking draws out their flavour and this can make the soup too strong.

3 Add enough liquid to cover, but if a concentrated stock is wanted, then use less liquid and cover the top with foil, then add the lid.

4 If making a meat soup cut the pieces into small cubes. The vegetables used should be very thinly sliced; carrots take some time to cook so should be put at the bottom of the slow cooker.

5 To shorten cooking time, first lightly sauté the bones, meat and vegetables in a little oil or fat, but do not let them colour, just soften slightly. Pour off excess oil before transferring to the cooker and covering with boiling liquid.

6 Thickening can be done either at the end using a little creamed cornflour or flour, or at the beginning by adding flour to the sautéed meat or vegetables in the frying pan, then gradually adding the stock and bringing to the boil, stirring until it is smooth, before putting it into the cooker.

7 Do not over-season, for again the flavour is enhanced by the slow cooking. Add a little to begin with, then taste again when cooking is completed.

8 Do not add milk until the last half-hour of cooking as it could separate. Cream, yoghurt or beaten egg yolks should be added just before serving, heated but not reboiled.

Stock

There are three basic meat or poultry stocks: brown stock, meat stock and white stock which is made from poultry and or veal bones. Fish stock which is used for sauces and soups is made from fish bones, skin and trimmings.

Brown stock is made by first putting the bones (with any vegetable trimmings) into a roasting pan, and then browning them in a hot oven (210°C, 420°F, gas 7) for about half an hour. Rub a little flour into the bones and proceed as below. Do not let the bones become burnt as this gives a bitter flavour.

Stock For meat or poultry bones. If a jellied stock is wanted, add either a veal knuckle bone, or a large split pig's foot.

Unless using this stock at once, do not add potato, turnip, parsnip or green vegetables.

Ingredients

approximately 1 kg (2¼ lb) raw or cooked meat or poultry bones, chopped or broken up
1 medium sliced onion

1 clove garlic
1 medium finely sliced carrot
1 stick finely chopped celery if available

a bouquet of fresh herbs (bayleaf, parsley, thyme, tarragon, etc.)
salt and freshly ground pepper

boiling water to cover
1 glass white wine or cider (optional)

Preheat the cooker to HIGH for 20–30 minutes. Put the vegetables on the bottom then the chopped bones on top with the herbs. Pour in enough boiling water to cover, but if adding the wine then make allowance for it. Cover with foil first if not over half-full, put on the lid and cook on LOW for at least 10 hours. This stock can be left for 12–15 hours without spoiling. Season to taste.

Strain and cool quickly, removing any fat when cold, or before using.

Fish stock Use within 24 hours if not freezing.

1 kg (2¼ lb) fish bones, trimmings, skin, etc.
bouquet of herbs including fennel if possible
salt and white freshly ground pepper
small piece of lemon peel or a squeeze of the juice

1 clove garlic
1 small onion, finely sliced
boiling water to cover
1 glass white wine or cider (optional)

Preheat cooker to HIGH for 20 minutes. Put the onion and chopped garlic at the bottom, then add the fish trimmings, lemon peel and herbs. Cover with boiling water and the wine if using. Cover with foil if not over half-full, and then the lid. Cook on LOW for about 8–10 hours, but further cooking will not spoil the stock. Season to taste.

Strain and cool quickly.

Note The different models of slow crockery pot cookers vary slightly in performance, so please read instructions fully, and choose a similar recipe for timing.

Note These recipes are for the 2.5–3 litre (5–6 pint) crock-pot, so halve ingredients if using smaller models.

Beef Goulash Soup with Dumplings

This is really a soup-stew and a delicious meal in itself.

Ingredients (serves 4–6)
2 tablespoons oil
450 g (1 lb) stewing steak, trimmed and cut into cubes
1 medium onion, finely chopped
2 medium carrots, shredded
1 stalk celery, finely chopped
2 medium leeks, finely chopped
1 tablespoon flour
salt and freshly ground pepper
3 peeled, chopped tomatoes or equivalent canned
1 teaspoon tomato purée
½ teaspoon caraway seeds

1 tablespoon paprika
1 bayleaf
stock to cover (stock cubes dissolved can be used)
1 tablespoon chopped parsley

For the dumplings
100 g (4 oz) self-raising flour
2 heaped tablespoons grated suet or margarine
a little water
1 tablespoon grated horseradish or creamed (optional)
salt

Preheat the cooker to HIGH for 20 minutes. First heat up the oil and quickly fry the meat cubes, then the vegetables. Sprinkle over the flour and the paprika and mix well. Moisten with a little stock, then add the caraway seeds, the tomatoes and tomato purée and mix well. Transfer to the cooker, cover with stock and add a little seasoning and the bayleaf. Cover and cook on HIGH for 30 minutes, then turn to LOW and cook for 6–8 hours or until meat is tender. Longer time will not spoil the soup.

See also *Hungarian Beef*, page 69.

To make the dumplings, rub the fat into the flour and add a pinch of salt; then pour in about 2 tablespoons of water to make a stiffish dough. With floured hands shape into small balls (they will swell a lot in cooking). Make a little hole in the middle of each and put in a little horseradish, squeezing together well to stop it coming out. Herbs can be used instead of horseradish if preferred. Turn up cooker to HIGH about an hour before the end of the cooking time and drop dumplings into the soup with a teaspoon. Garnish with chopped parsley before serving.

Cock-a-Leekie Soup

This is a famous traditional Scottish soup and a delicious way of using a boiling fowl. However, if one is not obtainable, then use chicken joints, or even leftover chicken. It makes a very good meal followed by cheese and fruit.

Important: Frozen chicken must be thoroughly thawed before using.

Ingredients (serves 6–8)
1 boiling fowl
2 rashers chopped bacon or
  leftover ham
10 medium leeks, cleaned
125 g (4 oz) cooked prunes
parsley for garnish

a mixed bouquet of parsley,
  thyme and a bayleaf
salt and freshly ground pepper
water or stock to cover
1 tablespoon cornflour or *beurre
  manié* (see below)

Turn cooker to HIGH while you are preparing the ingredients.
Skin and joint the bird, heat up the bacon and, when the fat is running out, sauté the chicken pieces until golden. You can bone the bird first and then boil up the bones and skin in 1 litre (1½ pints) water for half an hour, and use this strained stock instead of water. Chop the leeks very finely and put all the ingredients except the prunes, the cornflour and the parsley into the cooker, seeing that the stock or water covers them. Cover and cook on HIGH for 1 hour, then turn to LOW and cook for 8–10 hours. Half an hour before the end add the cooked prunes, turn to HIGH and finish cooking. Thicken at the same time with 1 level tablespoon cornflour creamed with a little water, or use a *beurre manié*, which is 1 teaspoon butter creamed with approximately 2 teaspoons flour or as much as can be absorbed by the butter. Add this in small pieces, and stir before putting back the lid.

If a shorter cooking time is desired then leave on HIGH for 4–5 hours. Garnish with plenty of fresh, chopped parsley before serving.

If only half a chicken is used and it is raw, the cooking time will be about the same, but if leftover chicken is used, the 1 hour can be taken off the cooking time, and it is not necessary to sauté the chicken.

Cream of Corn Soup

Ingredients (serves 6–8)
2 cans whole kernel corn (425 g or
  15 oz) or use fresh corn
1 small onion, finely chopped
1.5 litres (2 pints) chicken stock
  (cubes can be used)
1 cup mashed potato (made-up
  potato powder can be used)

pinch of paprika
pinch of nutmeg
salt and freshly ground pepper

To garnish
4 tablespoons cream and 1
  tablespoon finely chopped
  parsley

15

Turn the cooker to HIGH for 20 minutes. Mix together corn, onion, potato, paprika, nutmeg, salt and pepper and put into the cooker with the chicken stock. Cover and turn to LOW after 15 minutes and cook for 6–8 hours. Or cook on HIGH for 4–5 hours. Liquidize the soup if you like, and serve hot or chilled, garnished with a little cream and chopped parsley.

Dál Soup

This is an Indian soup and very warming on a cold day. If made with less water it can be used as a thick sauce over rice with hard-boiled eggs.

Ingredients (serves 6–8)
450 g (1 lb) orange lentils
2 heaped teaspoons sugar
¼ level teaspoon cinnamon or a
   small piece cinnamon bark
2 large fresh bayleaves
pinch of chilli powder
2 heaped teaspoons salt
2 level teaspoons turmeric

6 whole peppercorns
1 teaspoon garam masala or a good
   curry powder
1 medium onion, finely sliced
2 litres (3½ pints) boiling water

To garnish
1 medium-large onion fried in
   oil until crisp

Turn the cooker to HIGH for 20 minutes. Then put all ingredients into cooker and mix well. Cover with the boiling water, put the lid on and cook on HIGH for half an hour, then on LOW for 6–8 hours. Or on HIGH for 4–5 hours. Discard the bayleaves and peppercorns.

To serve, fry the sliced onion in the hot oil until it is crisp and golden brown, and scatter on the top.

To Make the Sauce Use only 1.8 litres (3 pints) and stir well after the first half hour.

Cooking time is the same as for the soup.

Fish Chowder

Ingredients (serves 4–6)
1 kg (2¼ lb) white fish (cod,
   haddock, coley, pollock, etc.)
1 tablespoon oil
2 rashers bacon, chopped
1 small sliced onion
1 chopped garlic clove
3 peeled potatoes, cut into small
   cubes or grated

4 medium peeled, chopped
   tomatoes
1 heaped teaspoon tomato purée
a squeeze of lemon juice
a bouquet of herbs, such as
   bayleaf, thyme and parsley
1.2 litres (2 pints) stock (see page
   13) or water
2 teaspoons Worcestershire sauce

a dash of sherry (optional)
salt and freshly ground pepper

To garnish
6 crushed cream cracker biscuits
or croûtons (see page 18)

Turn the cooker on to HIGH for 20 minutes. If you have the skin, bones, etc. of the fish, boil them up with about 600 ml (1 pint) water, salt and pepper and a sprig of parsley for about half an hour, then strain. Make sure frozen fish is well thawed out before using.

Cut the fish into pieces about 5 cm (2 in) square. Heat up the oil and fry the bacon in it, then put into the cooker and soften the onion, garlic and potato cubes in the fat. Add to the cooker, with the tomatoes, tomato purée, lemon juice, herbs and finally the stock or water. Stir well and season lightly. Cover and cook on HIGH for 3–4 hours or on LOW for 6–8 hours.

When cooked add the Worcestershire sauce and the sherry and taste for seasoning. Serve either with crushed cream cracker biscuits or croûtons.

Chicken and Prawn Gumbo

This is a succulent soup-stew perfected by Creole cooks in New Orleans. It is filling but also economical, for leftovers of poultry, fish, shellfish, meat or game can be used. Traditionally dried filé powder (which is made from the young, dried leaves of the sassafras tree and available from good delicatessens) is added when the soup has been taken from the heat. If reheated, the powder makes the stew stringy and uneatable. Okra, also known as Lady's Fingers, can be used instead and this is often available fresh or canned. Do not combine the two in the same dish, for the okra has a similar gummy property, but the flavour is blander. Nevertheless, a very good soup-stew can be made without using either. *Frozen chicken must be thoroughly thawed before using.*

Ingredients (serves 4–6)
1 small chicken, jointed, or legs
  and wings from cooked chicken
1 small can tomatoes, chopped
2 tablespoons chopped parsley
salt and freshly ground pepper
600 ml (1 pint) water or chicken
  stock
1 large chopped onion
1 finely chopped green or red
  pepper

2 stalks finely chopped celery
1 teaspoon filé powder or 1 small
  can okra (not essential)
3 tablespoons oil

To garnish
chopped parsley and 12 cooked
  Dublin Bay prawns

Turn cooker on to HIGH for 20 minutes. Heat up the oil and lightly fry the chicken, then transfer it to the cooker and in the same oil sauté the onion, sweet pepper and celery until soft. Mix these with the chicken pieces. Add the tomatoes and liquid, the okra (drained), the stock and seasonings. Cover and cook on HIGH for 4–5 hours or on LOW for 8–10 hours. Just before serving add the prawns and cover thickly with chopped parsley. If using the filé powder, then this is put into each plate (small pinch) and the hot soup is poured over and well stirred.

For a main meal serve with boiled, fluffy rice and green beans.

Split Pea Soup

Either yellow or green peas can be used, and the same recipe used for lentils, both the orange and the brown variety, but omit Worcestershire sauce.

Ingredients (serves 8)

450 g (1 lb) green or yellow split peas soaked for at least 4 hours
1 hambone with some meat left on, or 2 rashers chopped bacon
1 medium sliced onion
1 celery stalk, finely chopped, if available
1 bayleaf
2.5 litres (4 pints) water or to cover
salt and pepper
Worcestershire sauce

Turn the cooker on to HIGH for 20 minutes. Combine all ingredients in the cooker, cover and cook at LOW either overnight, or for at least 10 hours. Then lift out the hambone and take off any pieces of meat and return them to the cooker. Lift out bayleaf. Add about 1 teaspoon Worcestershire sauce and stir well.

To serve, either fry some bread quickly in hot oil, and cut up into croûtons, or for a more substantial meal add some chopped frankfurter sausages or small pieces of salami.

Variations

1 If using the brown lentils, some small leftover pieces of lamb make a pleasant change, and about 2 peeled and chopped tomatoes can be added.

2 If using the orange lentils, then the addition of 1 level tablespoon turmeric, 2 teaspoons curry powder and a pinch of ground coriander and nutmeg, makes a pleasant curry soup. See also *Dál*, page 16.

Oatmeal Soup

This is a Scottish speciality and has a very elusive and pleasant taste.

Ingredients (serves 4–6)

1 tablespoon butter or margarine
4 level tablespoons oatmeal
1.25 litres (2 pints) chicken stock
salt and freshly ground pepper
1 large, finely sliced onion
1 tablespoon chopped parsley
150 ml (¼ pint) cream

Turn the cooker to HIGH for 20 minutes. Meanwhile, heat the fat and lightly fry the onion until golden, then add the oatmeal and just let it soften. Put into the cooker, and add the boiling stock slowly, stirring all the time. Season, cover and cook on LOW for 4–5 hours or HIGH for 2–3 hours. Liquidize, reheat and serve with cream and chopped parsley.

Oatmeal and Leek Soup

This is a traditional Irish soup known as Brotchán Roy.

Ingredients (serves 4–6)

6 large leeks
1 heaped tablespoon butter or margarine
2 tablespoons flake oatmeal
1.25 litres (2 pints) chicken or ham stock
1 tablespoon chopped parsley
salt and freshly ground pepper
a little cream to garnish

Turn the cooker on to HIGH for 20 minutes. Prepare the leeks and cut them into chunks about 2.5 cm (1 in) long, leaving on a certain amount of the green part. Heat the butter and very lightly fry the leeks so they soften a little but do not brown. Put them into the cooker. Heat up the stock and add the oatmeal; when boiling pour over the leeks. Season to taste and stir well. Cover and cook on LOW for 6–8 hours or on HIGH for 4–6 hours. Thin down with milk if required.

Pour a little cream or top of the milk into each portion and sprinkle the chopped parsley over the top.

Philadelphia Pepperpot

This is an American favourite which comes from Philadelphia. Legend has it that Washington ordered a good soup to cheer his troops during the hard winter of 1777–8 and was told there was nothing but tripe, peppercorns, herbs, vegetables, a few scraps and bones. The cook improvised the following soup and called it after his home town. To make it even more filling, dumplings were added (see page 14). It has been popular ever since.

Ingredients (serves 6–8)

1 knuckle bone of veal or ham with some meat still on

450 g (1 lb) dressed tripe cut into 2.5 cm (1 in) squares

1 large onion, finely sliced

pinch of chilli powder

3 medium potatoes chopped finely

1 bayleaf, 2 sprigs thyme, 1 sprig parsley

$\frac{1}{2}$ teaspoon finely ground peppercorns

$\frac{1}{2}$ teaspoon whole allspice

pinch of dried oregano

boiling water or stock to cover

salt

Turn the cooker on to HIGH for 20 minutes. Put all ingredients into the cooker and stir well. Cover and cook overnight on LOW or for 4–6 hours on HIGH, but check that the tripe is tender. Take out the bone, remove any pieces of meat and put them back into the soup. If using dumplings, then put them in half an hour before the end and cook them on HIGH.

Variation If the tripe is omitted and 3 large, chopped and peeled tomatoes and 1 finely chopped green or red pepper are added, it becomes *Creole Soup*.

Scotch Broth

This famous soup also called Barley Broth is a meal in itself and very comforting on a cold day. Other vegetables according to season can be added, such as peas, beans, celery, etc.

Ingredients (serves 6–8)

450 g (1 lb) lean mutton or lamb, (neck is good for this) cubed

1.8 litres (3 pints) water

2 turnips finely chopped

2 medium carrots, finely chopped

1 large sliced onion

white of 1 leek chopped finely

25 g (1 oz) pearl barley

1 bayleaf and pinch of rosemary

salt and freshly ground pepper

2 tablespoons chopped parsley

Turn the cooker to HIGH while preparing the soup. Trim the meat of fat or gristle, then put it into a saucepan with the bayleaf, water and boil it for 20 minutes, removing the scum from the top. Then put into the cooker all the ingredients (vegetables at the bottom) omitting half the parsley. Cover and cook on LOW for 8–10 hours or on HIGH for 5–6 hours. Garnish with the rest of the parsley before serving.

Fish

Fish cooked in the usual manner does not take very long, so why use the slow cooker ? There are several good reasons, one being that slow cooking develops rather than destroys its delicate flavour. Another is that all its nutritive values are enclosed, and the fish both tastes good and keeps its maximum food value. There is no fear of it breaking up as sometimes happens when cooking in the ordinary way, and another great thing in its favour is that the smell is contained and does not permeate throughout the house.

There are one or two points which should be followed in slow fish cooking:

1 Most important, if the fish is frozen, it *must* be thoroughly thawed before cooking.

2 It is wise to lightly grease the base of the cooker first.

3 LOW cooking is advised for thin white-fish fillets, but a firm fish such as mackerel or fish steaks can also be cooked on HIGH.

4 The cooker should always be preheated on HIGH for about 20 minutes. The following recipes fall into two categories: those which can be cooked and eaten straight away, hot, and those which are usually served cold, such as potted herrings.

The latter dishes make excellent first courses and can be cooked ahead of time and put into the dish they will be served from. Naturally the others can also be served as a first course, and all fears are allayed as to whether they will be over-cooked by keeping hot.

Thirdly, they all make very good dishes for a luncheon or a light meal.

Casserole of Spiced Fish
Almost any thick white fish can be used for this dish such as bass, sea bream, cod, coley, hake, haddock, whiting, John Dory, etc.

Ingredients (serves 4–6)

1 kg (2¼ lb) filleted and skinned white fish

1 glass white wine, approximately 6 tablespoons

1 small stick celery, finely chopped

450 g (1 lb) peeled and chopped tomatoes or equivalent can

1 small onion, finely sliced

50 g (2 oz) mushrooms

1 tablespoon chopped parsley

sprig of fresh fennel or ½ teaspoon fennel seeds

2 tablespoons pine kernels (optional)

1 crushed garlic clove

½ teaspoon ground coriander

½ teaspoon ground nutmeg

½ teaspoon cayenne pepper

salt and freshly ground pepper

Turn the cooker to HIGH for 20 minutes. See that the fish is quite free of bones, rub it all over with a little salt, and marinate it in the wine for 20 minutes. Meanwhile finely chop or slice all the vegetables and put the celery in first, a layer of mushrooms, the onion, then some of the tomatoes. If using canned tomatoes, drain them first. Chop up the garlic and crush it well and sprinkle this over the tomatoes and season each layer with a little salt. Take the fish from the marinade, pat it dry, rub in the ground spices on both sides, lay it on top of the vegetables, and scatter the pine kernels over if using.

Mix the fennel and half the parsley with the rest of the tomatoes, then cover the fish with the remaining mushrooms, finishing with the tomatoes. Gently pour over the wine, and if using canned tomatoes, about half the juice, otherwise see that the wine comes up to half the casserole. Cover and cook on LOW for 4–6 hours or on HIGH for 3–4 hours. Sprinkle with the remaining parsley before serving.

Note If using one of the larger crock-pots and the ingredients do not come over half-full, put a layer of foil over the top before adding the lid.

Cod in Cider

Other thick white fish can also be used such as hake, haddock, etc.

Ingredients (serves 4–6)

1 tablespoon butter or margarine

3 medium leeks, finely sliced

½ finely sliced fennel bulb if available, or ½ teaspoon fennel seeds or 2 chopped fresh leaves

225 g (½ lb) finely sliced mushrooms

4 or 6 cod steaks

2 tablespoons lemon juice and the grated rind of 1 lemon

1 bayleaf

150 ml (¼ pint) cider

Turn the cooker to HIGH for 20 minutes and lightly butter the base.

Put half the finely chopped leeks, the fennel and half the mushrooms on the bottom, season, and put the fish on top, pouring over the lemon juice, grated rind and seasoning to taste. Put the remaining vegetables on top, putting the bayleaf in first, and ending with the mushrooms. Pour the cider over and cook on LOW for 3–4 hours, or on HIGH for 2–3 hours.

Note If the vegetables are still firm then increase cooking time on LOW to 4–6 hours and on HIGH to 3–4 hours. The latter times are better for the crock-pot that can be lifted out of the base, for the cooking elements are mainly on the bottom, and the vegetables will cook more quickly if they are all put on the bottom and the fish steaks on the top.

Variation The leeks can be omitted and 3 tablespoons cream added half an hour before serving, the cooker turned to HIGH.

Cod Creole

Also for other thick white fish such as haddock, hake, etc.

Ingredients (serves 4–6)

1 tablespoon butter or margarine
4 or 6 fillets of cod or cod steaks
1 small red or green sweet pepper
1 bayleaf
pinch of dried or fresh basil
salt

1 crushed garlic clove
½ teaspoon brown sugar
grated rind of 1 orange
1 can tomatoes (425 g or 15 oz size)
3 drops Tabasco sauce or a pinch of chilli powder

Turn the cooker to HIGH for 20 minutes. Grease the cooker with about half the butter or margarine. Put the bayleaf on the bottom with the finely sliced and seeded sweet pepper. Lay the fish on the top and season to taste. Mix the tomatoes which have been coarsely chopped with the grated orange rind, the brown sugar, crushed garlic and the basil, and add a little salt and the Tabasco sauce or chilli powder. Pour this carefully over the top of the fish, and dot with the rest of the butter.

If the cooker is only half-full cover with foil before adding the lid. Cook on HIGH for 15 minutes, then on LOW for 4–6 hours.

Baked Whitefish with Grapefruit and Grapes

Almost any white fish can be used for this pleasantly fresh-tasting dish. Cod, haddock, hake, coley, monkfish, bass, etc., and either fillets or steaks can be used.

Ingredients (serves 4–6)
1 tablespoon butter
4 or 6 fish fillets or steaks
100 g (4 oz) seeded white or black
  grapes

1 large grapefruit or a small can
1 teaspoon light brown sugar
salt
water, white wine or cider if using
  fresh grapefruit

Turn the cooker to HIGH for 20 minutes. Use half the butter to grease the bottom of the cooker, lay the fish fillets on top and salt lightly. Put the grapefruit segments and the grapes on top having first mixed the brown sugar with them. If using canned grapefruit add half the juice and if using fresh grapefruit add about 3 tablespoons water or, if you prefer, white wine or cider. Cover with foil if using a 3–3.5 litre (5–6 pint) cooker, add the lid, and cook on HIGH for 15 minutes, then on LOW for 3–4 hours.

Curried Fish

Make the *Curry Sauce* on page 38, and add the fish cut into 5 cm (2 in) pieces, or use leftover cooked fish or prawns or shrimps or a mixture. If using cooked fish it can be added for the last half hour of cooking with the cooker turned to HIGH. Raw chunks of fish should be added and cooked on LOW for 2–3 hours.

Smoked Haddock Savoy*

Although smoked haddock is used in this nineteenth-century dish which originated at the Savoy Hotel, London, other cooked fish such as poached hake, haddock, cod, salmon, etc. can also be used.

Ingredients (serves 3–4)
1 large cooked, smoked haddock
  or 350 g (12 oz) other cooked fish
600 ml (1 pint) creamy milk

2 tablespoons grated, hard cheese
  such as Parmesan
3 eggs
salt and cayenne pepper

Turn the cooker to HIGH for 20 minutes. Then see that you have either a small trivet which will fit in the bottom of your deep cooker, or something like a jam jar lid.

Fillet and flake the fish and mix it with the grated cheese and seasonings. Beat the eggs, warm the milk without boiling it, and pour it over the eggs, stirring well. Pour this over the fish and cheese

* If you have the removable stoneware pot type of slow cooker this custard can be cooked in it and the pot brought to table. If using the fixed-pot variety it is better to put the custard into a smaller basin or soufflé-type dish which will fit in and surround it with water. (See method.) This dish can then be brought to table.

and mix well. Then pour this into the basin which fits into the cooker and cover with foil. Boil up some water, stand the basin on the trivet or lid and pour the boiling water around to come up to half-way up the side of the basin. Put the lid on and cook on LOW for 4 hours, or until a knife inserted in the centre comes out clean.

Fish Soufflé or Fiskegratin

This is a Danish recipe and is really a soufflé without tears. It is very good with fresh or canned salmon.

Ingredients (serves 4–6)
50 g (2 oz) butter or margarine
50 g (2 oz) flour
300 ml (½ pint) milk or fish stock

2 large or 3 small separated eggs
225 g (8 oz) cooked, flaked fish
salt and freshly ground pepper

Turn the cooker to HIGH for 20 minutes. Heat the butter in a saucepan, add the flour and let it cook for 1 minute. Add the milk or stock and stir until smooth, and simmer for about 2 minutes. Let it cool, then stir in the beaten egg yolks gradually.

Add the flaked fish and season to taste. Beat the egg whites until stiff and fold in, seeing that they go right to the bottom. Grease a dish which will fit into your cooker, or put straight into the greased cooker, making sure that the mixture only comes to two thirds of the way up the sides. If using a basin covered with foil, stand it on a trivet or a jam jar lid as above and pour boiling water to half-way up. Cover and cook on LOW for 4 hours. Serve either with a white sauce to which grated cheese has been added or a mushroom sauce.

This recipe can be used with ham and/or chicken, cheese, crab, or spinach.

Variation The mixture can also be put in small individual pots, covered with foil and standing on a trivet with boiling water to half-way up. The cooking time is reduced to LOW for 3 hours.

Indian Plaice

Ingredients (serves 4)
25 g (1 oz) butter or margarine
4 fillets plaice or lemon sole
75 g (3 oz) cooked rice
1½ teaspoons curry powder, or to taste
2 tablespoons water or fish stock (see page 13)

1 tablespoon chopped fresh herbs such as parsley, fennel, chives
4 rounds of chopped pineapple
2 tablespoons pineapple juice
salt and freshly ground pepper

To garnish
4 rounds pineapple

Turn the cooker to HIGH for 20 minutes. Grease the bottom and lower sides of the cooker well. Skin the fillets on both sides if there is black skin, and lay them out flat. Mix together the rice, curry powder, chopped fresh herbs, finely chopped pineapple, the rest of the butter, salt and pepper. Put a good spoonful on each fillet, roll them up and put them fold-side downwards in the cooker. Or you can tie them with cotton twine. Lay them closely together in the cooker, and pour the pineapple juice and water around.

Put the lid on, adding a layer of foil if the contents do not come above half-way. Cook on LOW for 6–8 hours or on HIGH for 3–4 hours. Remove the twine before serving.

Note 6 or 8 fillets can be used but in that case increase the ingredients by one third. Cooking time remains the same.

Herrings cook very well in the crockery pot and there are many ways of doing them.

Baked Stuffed Herrings in Cider

Ingredients (serves 4)

4 large cleaned herrings
4 slices crustless bread soaked in a little milk
1 small finely chopped onion
grated rind and juice of ½ lemon
1 tablespoon chopped parsley
1 small peeled and grated apple
1 egg
salt and freshly ground pepper
a little butter or margarine
300 ml (½ pint) cider

Note 4 tablespoons of made-up parsley and thyme stuffing mix can be used. Turn the cooker to HIGH for 20 minutes. See that the fish are filleted and take particular care to cut away the side rib bones. Then mash up the soaked bread and mix together all the other ingredients except the cider. Fill each fish with the stuffing and secure with a cocktail stick or cotton twine. Lightly grease the bottom of the cooker, and lay the fish closely together, fold-side down. Heat the cider, pour it around, and cover with foil if not above the half-way mark. Then put on the lid and cook on LOW for 4–6 hours or on HIGH for 2–3 hours.

Mackerel can also be cooked the same way.

Herrings Baked in Tea

This is a Cornish recipe of the last century and gives the fish a most delicate taste. Mackerel are also very good cooked this way.

Ingredients (serves 4)
4 cleaned and opened herrings or
   mackerel
4 bayleaves
10 black peppercorns

1 tablespoon brown sugar
300 ml ($\frac{1}{2}$ pint) of equal parts of
   white vinegar and milkless tea
salt

Turn the cooker to HIGH for 20 minutes. Then put a bayleaf into each fish and lay side by side in the cooker. Sprinkle each fish with a little salt and the brown sugar. Heat up the vinegar and cold tea and when hot pour this around. Cover with foil if it does not come above the half-way mark, add the lid, and cook on LOW for 4–6 hours or HIGH for 2–3 hours. They should be eaten cold with a little of the juice.

Note The more usual method of using only vinegar can be done as above with the addition of a spoonful of pickling spices.

Jamaica 'Trouts'

This is an eighteenth-century recipe for herrings from *A Heritage of British Cooking* by Maggie Black. It is also good for small mackerel. The name 'Jamaica' comes from the allspice used, for Jamaica pepper is an alternative name.

Ingredients (serves 6–8)
6 or 8 cleaned and scaled herrings
   with the heads removed*

salt as needed
10–15 whole allspice berries
white wine vinegar as needed

First lay the herrings side by side in a square or oblong dish and sprinkle well with salt. Repeat until you have used all the fish, cover and leave in a cold place for 24 hours.

Turn the cooker to HIGH for 20 minutes.

Take out the herrings, wipe the surface dry and leave them to dry slightly. Put into the cooker, sprinkling with the allspice berries, and completely cover with the vinegar. Cover with the lid and cook at LOW for 8–10 hours or even longer if convenient. When cold take off any fat, and serve cold.

* If you have the large-size cooker then double quantities can be used. They will keep in a cold place for about 10–12 days.

West Country Baked Mackerel or Pilchards

Herrings can also be used.

Ingredients (serves 6)

6 small mackerel or fresh pilchards
1 medium sliced onion
1 teaspoon each ground cloves and allspice
4 bayleaves
300 ml (½ pint) each pale beer and white vinegar
black pepper and salt

Turn the cooker to HIGH for 20 minutes. Salt and spice each fish, roll them and lay in the cooker. Scatter on the finely sliced onion and bayleaves with plenty of black pepper. Pour on the heated vinegar and beer, cover and cook on LOW for 4–6 hours, or on HIGH for 2–3 hours.

Variation Use half Guinness and half vinegar.

Mackerel with Gooseberries and Fennel

Ingredients (serves 4–6)

4 mackerel, cleaned and filleted
4 sprigs fresh fennel or 1 teaspoon dried
4 thin slices lemon
100 g (4 oz) gooseberries
1 cup dry cider or dry white wine
salt and freshly ground pepper

Turn the cooker to HIGH for 20 minutes. Make sure that the mackerel are well filleted, then tuck a sprig of fresh fennel into each one with a few chopped gooseberries. (If using very tart gooseberries add a little brown sugar.) Add salt and pepper and put the rest of the gooseberries around the fish. Pour in the cider or wine. Lay a slice of lemon on top of each fish, cover with foil if the cooker is not above half-way, then the lid. Cook on LOW for 4–6 hours or HIGH for 2–3 hours.

This dish is delicious either hot or cold.

Variations

1 In the West Country of England, chopped rhubarb is used in place of the gooseberries.

2 If a tart flavour is liked, use half white wine vinegar and half water instead of the cider or wine.

Mackerel with Orange

Ingredients (serves 4)

4 mackerel, cleaned
1 large orange
1 small finely sliced onion
2 tablespoons fresh breadcrumbs
1 tablespoon chopped parsley

salt and pepper   1 small grated apple
300 ml (½ pint) cider or white wine

Turn the cooker to HIGH for 20 minutes. Finely grate the zest of the orange on to a large plate, quarter it and carve out the flesh and coarsely chop it. Mix with the breadcrumbs, finely chopped onion, apple and the parsley. Season well and fill the fish with this stuffing. Put into the cooker, and add the heated cider or wine. Cover with foil if not above the half-way mark, and the lid. Cook on LOW for 4–6 hours or on HIGH for 2–3 hours.

Variation Lemon can be used instead of orange.

Cape Cod Mackerel

This method is also good with cod steaks or bass.

Ingredients (serves 4)

4 mackerel, cleaned
1 small can concentrated orange
  juice

3 tablespoons soy sauce
1 heaped tablespoon brown sugar
2 tablespoons butter or margarine

Turn the cooker to HIGH for 20 minutes. Grease the bottom of the cooker and heat up all the other ingredients including the rest of the butter in a small saucepan. Put the fish in the cooker and pour the hot liquid over and around. Cover with foil if not above the half-way mark, add the lid and cook on LOW for 4–6 hours or on HIGH for 2–3 hours. Serve hot.

Trout Baked

Ingredients (serves 4–6)

1 teaspoon butter
4 trout, cleaned
4 thin slices lemon
3 tablespoons double cream
a little flour

175 g (6 oz) sliced mushrooms
150 ml (¼ pint) dry white wine
salt and freshly ground white
  pepper
50 g (2 oz) blanched, sliced
  almonds (optional)

Turn the cooker to HIGH for 20 minutes. Season the trout and lightly roll in flour, then grease the cooker with the butter. Put half the sliced mushrooms on the bottom, then the fish, with the remaining mushrooms on top. Pour the wine over, and put a lemon slice on each fish.

Cover with foil if it does not come above the half-way mark, then the lid. Cook on LOW for 4–6 hours or HIGH for 2–3 hours. Fifteen minutes before it is ready stir in the cream, and cook on HIGH for

15 minutes. Meanwhile toss the almonds in a hot pan without anything else until they turn golden brown. Serve the fish with the toasted almonds scattered on top.

Sole can also be cooked in this way.

Trout Potted

This is an eighteenth-century recipe which is very good. Herrings can also be done this way. They will keep in a cold place for about 2 weeks providing they are quite covered with the melted butter. Halve ingredients for the 1.8 litre (3 pint) crock-pot.

Ingredients
8–10 trout, cleaned
a little vinegar
salt and pepper

a pinch of ground mace or nutmeg
100 g (4 oz) butter plus
    75 g (3 oz) butter

To prepare the fish, wash them in a little vinegar, and open them, cutting off the heads and tails. Season quite thickly with salt and pepper and leave covered for 3 hours, or more if possible.

Turn the cooker to HIGH for 20 minutes. Lightly grease the cooker with butter, and put in the drained fish side by side, head to tail. Add the 100 g (4 oz) butter cut into small pieces, and the spices, cover with foil if they do not come over half-way up, then the lid and cook on LOW for 4–6 hours or HIGH for 2–3 hours. When cooked pour off the buttery juices (which can be used as a fish sauce if frozen), put side by side into a clean dish and let them cool quickly. Then heat up the rest of the butter and pour evenly over so that it covers the fish completely. Keep cold until serving, with buttered brown bread, and with grated orange or lemon peel in it.

They make a delicious first course, or a light luncheon with salad made from chopped apple, celery and a few sultanas, mixed with a French dressing.

Tuna Fish Loaf

Ingredients (serves about 4)
1 can tuna fish (200 g or 7 oz)
1 can sweet corn (350 g or 12 oz)
1 teaspoon butter
2 peeled and chopped tomatoes

1 small can (212 g or 7½ oz) cream
    mushrooms
a tablespoon chopped parsley
salt and pepper
2 beaten eggs

Turn the cooker to HIGH for 20 minutes, and lightly grease the bottom with the butter. If your cooker is the deeper kind, find a 1 litre (1½ pint) dish and grease that. Have ready a small trivet or a jam jar lid. Drain the fish and the corn and mix with the chopped tomatoes, the parsley and season to taste. Beat the eggs and mix well into the creamed mushrooms, beating them together. Pour this over the fish and corn mixture, mixing well. Put into the cooker or the dish (if you are using a dish cover it with foil). Stand it on the trivet and pour boiling water around to half-way up. Cover and cook on LOW for 4–6 hours or HIGH for 2–3 hours. The cooking time is the same if the mixture is put straight into the cooker.

Cool quickly, and serve cut into slices with a salad of either raw or cooked vegetables.

Variation Use cooked and flaked smoked haddock or smoked cod. Use cooked rice instead of the corn and add 50 g (2 oz) of a hard grated cheese. The latter recipe can be done with almost any cooked, firm white fish as well as the tuna, or drained canned salmon.

Yorkshire Herring Pie

This is very similar to a Russian recipe which is very good served with dollops of natural, plain yoghurt on top, and a beetroot salad. Or you can use the yoghurt as a dressing for the sliced beetroots, which can be mixed with a little chopped, raw apple.

Ingredients (serves 4)

4 fresh, filleted herrings
4 medium size half-cooked
  potatoes
2 small to medium apples
salt and freshly ground pepper
1 small sliced onion or shallot
1 tablespoon chopped parsley
25 g (1 oz) butter
150 ml (¼ pint) water

Turn the cooker to HIGH for 20 minutes, then lightly grease the bottom. Cut the fish fillets into three and soak in salted water for 15 minutes. Drain and pat dry. Slice the part-cooked potatoes thinly and line the cooker with a layer, then add a layer of finely sliced apple and a little onion or shallot. Season to taste, and put the herrings on top with the parsley. Finish with the rest of the potatoes, onion, and seasoning. Add the butter in little pieces, the water, then cover with foil if does not come to half-way up the cooker. Add the lid, and cook on LOW for 4–6 hours or HIGH for 3–4 hours.

Note If using the lift-out pot type of cooker the potatoes can be browned under a grill, or in the oven, and if liked the top can be sprinkled first with grated cheese.

See also *Fish Chowder*, page 16.

Poultry and Game

POULTRY

All poultry and game cook very well in the crockery pot. Generally they do not take as long as meat, but can be left on LOW for an hour more at least without spoiling. Tougher, older birds are tenderized by the slow cooking, and of course, all the flavour will be retained.

Some vegetables, such as carrot and celery, may take longer than the bird to cook unless cut very finely, but this can be avoided by putting them on the bottom of the cooker and seeing that they are covered by the water or stock.

Chicken is the obvious choice for many of the recipes, but duck and turkey joints also cook extremely well. If the duck is fatty, there are some precautions you take to avoid this which can be found on page 45.

There are a few general rules which should be followed when cooking poultry or game.

1 *Most important*: It is vital that all poultry and game is thoroughly thawed out if frozen. If this is not done it is possible that the low heat of the cooker multiplies rather than kills any bacteria present, so make quite certain that it is completely thawed before starting to cook.

2 Then wash and dry the bird and season inside and out.

3 It is wiser in some cases to brown the bird in a little oil or butter, before putting into the pot, but this instruction will be part of the recipe.

4 Each kind of cooker varies slightly both in size and cooking methods, so look for a similar recipe given in your booklet and follow instructions given there.

5 Whole birds can be roasted in the cooker, but do check that the

lid of the pot fits properly. If it is not seated correctly, cut the bird in half or into serving joints. The bird will not cook in the stated time if this is not done.

Arroz con Pollo
This is a Spanish recipe for chicken with rice and vegetables, and makes an entire meal without any additions. Duck portions can also be used, but prick the skin all over and brown in oil first.

Ingredients (serves 4)

1–1.25 kg (2½–3 lb) roasting chicken cut into joints
1 clove chopped garlic
1 small chopped onion
1 medium seeded red or green pepper or equivalent canned
2 tablespoons medium sherry
200 g (7 oz) long grain rice*
pinch of saffron, optional

50 g (2 oz) chopped ham, bacon or salami
1 litre (1½ pints) chicken stock, or use stock cubes
4 peeled, sliced tomatoes or equivalent can
275 g (10 oz) peas or beans (if using frozen see they are thawed)
75 g (3 oz) olives, optional
salt and freshly ground pepper

Turn the cooker to HIGH for 20 minutes. Rub the chicken joints all over with salt and pepper then put all ingredients except the rice and peas into the cooker, seeing that the onion and chopped pepper are on the bottom. Cover and cook on LOW for 6–8 hours, or HIGH for 4 hours. Turn to HIGH 1 hour before serving and add the rice and peas, stir well, cover and continue cooking for 1 hour.

Variations

1 If using the cooked rice, take out the chicken pieces and remove all the meat before adding it. Put the meat back with the rice and peas, having turned the cooker to HIGH when the chicken is taken out.

2 Mushrooms and 2 teaspoons tomato purée can be also added, but make certain the purée is mixed in well.

Baked or Roast Chicken
1 If using frozen chicken make certain it is thoroughly thawed.

2 Make sure that your slow cooker is big enough to take the whole bird, otherwise cut in half, or into serving pieces.

* Cooked rice (2 cups) can be used if preferred. Add with the peas and cook on HIGH for half an hour.

Ingredients

1.5–2 kg (3–4 lb) whole roasting chicken

1 cup bread and herb stuffing, optional

1 tablespoon butter

pinch dried tarragon

salt and freshly ground pepper

Turn the cooker to HIGH for 20 minutes, and lightly grease it. Wash the bird and dry with kitchen paper, and rub inside and out with salt and pepper. If using stuffing, prepare and stuff the bird, and secure it well. Cover the breast with the rest of the butter and sprinkle the tarragon over, then put into the cooker, cover and cook on HIGH for 4–6 hours, checking at minimum cooking time. Remove carefully and serve.

If you like a browner bird, sauté it all over in about 2 tablespoons oil before putting in the cooker.

Note This is a good method of cooking chicken to serve cold. Take all the meat from the bones when cooled a little, and use for a chicken mayonnaise or for a curry.

Chicken Cacciatora (*Pollo alla Cacciatora*)

This is 'Hunter's' chicken and a favourite Italian dish which is often made with tomato purée (and where would the hunters get that?) which detracts from the fresh flavour of the bird. This is also a good way to cook rabbit. If using frozen chicken make quite certain it is thoroughly thawed.

Ingredients (serves 4)

3 tablespoons oil, preferably olive

6 chicken portions, floured

2 garlic cloves

2 teaspoons chopped rosemary

1 bayleaf

salt and freshly ground pepper

1 medium onion, finely chopped

1 tablespoon fresh parsley

2 celery stalks with leaves, finely chopped

½ teaspoon celery salt

150 ml (¼ pint) dry white wine

salt and freshly ground pepper

Turn the cooker to HIGH for 20 minutes. Heat the oil and quickly fry the chicken pieces until golden. Put aside and fry the finely chopped onion, garlic, and chopped celery. Put the bayleaf, then the onion and celery at the bottom of the cooker, season, then the floured and sautéed chicken on top, with the herbs and seasonings. Pour the wine over, cover and cook on LOW for 8–10 hours or on HIGH for 4–5 hours.

Variation Add 100 g (4 oz) chopped mushrooms and 4 peeled and sliced tomatoes. Red wine can be used instead of white if preferred, and a small amount of chopped green or red sweet pepper can be added and should be put at the bottom of the cooker.

Chinese Chicken

Ingredients (serves 6)
6 large chicken joints, well thawed
salt and pepper
piece of green ginger* about 2.5 cm (1 in) long, chopped finely, or ½ teaspoon ground ginger
1 chopped clove garlic
1 tablespoon chopped green onion
450 ml (¾ pint) chicken stock

175 g (6 oz) approximately bean sprouts
100 g (4 oz) sliced water chestnuts or mushrooms
2 tablespoons sliced bamboo shoot, optional
1 tablespoon wine vinegar
2 tablespoons cornflour
2 tablespoons soy sauce

Turn the cooker to HIGH for 20 minutes. Wipe the chicken pieces well, remove the skin and rub with salt and pepper. Mix the stock with the garlic and ginger. Put the sliced bamboo shoots, water chestnuts and half the mushrooms on the bottom, put the chicken on top and cover with the remaining vegetables, then pour the stock over. Cover and cook on HIGH for 15 minutes, then on LOW for 6–8 hours. Mix the cornflour with the vinegar and when creamed add the soy sauce. Turn cooker to HIGH and stir into the chicken and stock. Cover and cook on HIGH for 15–20 minutes or until the sauce is slightly thickened.

Serve with either boiled or fried rice or with noodles.

See also *Beef and Green Ginger Casserole*, page 68.

Chicken Contadini

Pollo alla Contadini is another Italian recipe used a lot in the country districts.

Ingredients (serves 6)
4 tablespoons oil
6–8 chicken joints, well thawed if frozen
2 medium onions
4 tablespoons dark Italian vermouth

1 level teaspoon ground cinnamon
1 tablespoon tomato purée
450 ml (¾ pint) chicken stock
salt and a pinch cayenne pepper

Turn the cooker to HIGH for 20 minutes. Heat up the oil and quickly fry the chicken joints on all sides until golden. Put aside and sauté

* Obtainable from Oriental grocers or in cans.

the onions until soft. Put back the chicken, season to taste, then pour over the vermouth and set fire to it.

Add the tomato purée, cinnamon and stock, let it bubble up and transfer to the cooker. Cover and cook on LOW for 6–8 hours or on HIGH for 3–4 hours.

Country Chicken Casserole
Also good for rabbit.

Ingredients (serves 6)
2.5 kg (3 lb) chicken, cut into joints
1 litre (1½ pints) chicken stock
4 peeled, chopped tomatoes or equivalent can
350 g (12 oz) shelled broad beans, if using frozen see they are thawed

1 finely sliced onion
175 g (6 oz) boiling bacon, cut in cubes, or 4 streaky rashers
1 eating apple, cored, peeled and sliced
1 teaspoon sugar
pinch of savory
pinch of tarragon
salt and pepper

Turn the cooker to HIGH for 20 minutes. Put the chopped bacon into a pan and fry until crisp, transfer to the cooker and put the sliced onion and apple on top. Season lightly, omitting salt if the bacon is salty. Put the chicken joints on top with the savoury, sugar and tarragon. Pour the stock (warmed) over, cover and cook on HIGH for 15 minutes, then on LOW for 3–4 hours or until chicken is tender. At this point you may take the flesh from the bones and put it back in the cooker. Taste for seasoning and add the tomatoes and beans. Cover, turn to HIGH and cook for 1 hour.

Variation Use cider instead of stock. You could also add 4 medium, sliced potatoes, with the ingredients at the beginning. Cream can also be added, about 3 tablespoons, 10 minutes before the dish is ready.

Courgettes and Chicken

Ingredients (serves 6)
6 chicken joints, if frozen thaw thoroughly
2 tablespoons flour
salt and freshly ground pepper
3 tablespoons oil

½ teaspoon chopped tarragon
1 teaspoon butter
450 g (1 lb) sliced courgettes
½ teaspoon chopped basil
1 small sliced onion
300 ml (½ pint) chicken stock

Turn the cooker to HIGH for 20 minutes. Mix the salt and pepper into the flour and roll the chicken joints in this. If you prefer you can skin and bone the joints, in which case put them on to boil with seasonings and water to cover, so that by the time you have prepared the dish you will have chicken stock to use in this recipe.

Heat up the oil and quickly fry the joints until golden all over, take them out and reserve. Rub the cooker with the butter, and put the thinly sliced courgettes on the bottom mixed with the finely chopped onion. Season to taste and add the basil. Cover with the heated chicken stock, and put the chicken joints on top sprinkled with the chopped tarragon.

Cook on HIGH for 15 minutes, then turn to LOW and continue cooking for 6–8 hours, or for 3–4 on HIGH.

Variations
1 If using the lift-out pot type of cooker, the top can finally be sprinkled with grated Parmesan cheese and put under the grill or in the oven to brown.

2 Add 1 sliced aubergine, 1 or 2 chopped garlic cloves, 1 finely chopped sweet pepper, and 4 peeled and chopped tomatoes and you have a ratatouille with the chicken on top. Or you could soften these vegetables in oil before putting on the bottom of the pot and covering with the stock.

Chicken Curry

Ingredients (serves 6)
6–8 chicken joints, well thawed if frozen
2 tablespoons flour
1 teaspoon ground ginger
3–4 tablespoons oil
2 medium onions finely sliced
1 bayleaf
salt
1 tablespoon garam masala (obtainable from Oriental grocers)
2 teaspoons curry powder, or to taste
1 heaped teaspoon each of ground coriander and cardamom
4 peeled, chopped tomatoes or equivalent can, drained
barely 600 ml (1 pint) stock or water
1 small carton plain yoghurt (optional)

Turn the cooker to HIGH for 20 minutes. Mix together the ginger and the flour and roll the chicken joints in this. Heat the oil and fry the thinly sliced onions until just soft, but not coloured, and add the bayleaf. Put into the bottom of the cooker, then quickly fry the chicken joints in the same oil, all over. Sprinkle the curry powder and all the other spices over the top, add the tomatoes and also the stock. Let it just bubble up and put into the cooker, seeing that the liquid covers the onions on the bottom.

Cover and cook on HIGH for 15 minutes, then on LOW for 6–8 hours, or HIGH for 3–4 hours. If using the yoghurt, mix it in and turn cooker to HIGH and cook for 15–20 minutes. Serve with rice, mango chutney, poppadoms and a RAITA (see below).

This makes a pleasantly fragrant but mild curry: if you like it hotter, add more curry at the beginning and also a pinch of chilli powder. If you have not used the yoghurt, serve with a good squeeze of lemon juice.

Variations

1 Use either lamb, or beef cut into cubes, but increase cooking time to 8–10 hours on LOW and 4–5 hours on HIGH. Fish can be used, see page 24.

2 The tomatoes can be omitted.

Curry Sauce Make the sauce as above without any poultry, fish or meat, and cook on LOW for 4–6 hours, or HIGH for 2–3 hours. Double quantities will take the same time.

Raita These are pleasant accompaniments to any curry, and can be made from sliced banana, cucumber or onion. Whatever is chosen, slice thinly and mix with plain yoghurt, and a pinch of salt and cayenne pepper or chilli powder, but do not make it too hot, for it is the cold, refreshing taste which is a good contrast to the curry.

Chicken with Honey and Almonds

This dish is very easily done in the type of cooker which has the removable pot, but it can also be cooked in the other type.

Ingredients (serves 6)

6–8 chicken joints or whole chicken, about 1.5 kg (3 lb). Thaw well if frozen
1 lemon
2–3 tablespoons oil
2 medium, sliced onions

salt and pepper
300 ml (½ pint) cider, white wine or stock
4 tablespoons warm honey
50 g (2 oz) blanched, split almonds

First turn the cooker to HIGH for 20 minutes. Cut the lemon and squeeze out the juice, then rub the peel all over the chicken or chicken pieces. Heat up the oil and quickly fry the chicken until golden, season, then reserve. Finely slice the onions and put into the pot, and season to taste. Add the cider, wine or stock, and put the chicken pieces on top. Pour the lemon over, cover and cook at HIGH for 15 minutes, then on LOW for 6–8 hours, or HIGH for 3–4 hours.

Have the warmed honey ready and also the almonds which you have tossed in a hot pan without anything else (for their oil will cook them) until they are just a golden brown. If using a removable crockery pot, take it out, and brush the warmed honey over the top of the chicken, scatter the almonds over the top and put into a hot oven (220°C, 425°F, gas 7) at the top for about 15–20 minutes. If using the fixed crockery pot, lift out the chicken pieces and lay them on a foil-lined grill pan. Brush them with the honey and grill until the tops are golden. Brush at least twice with the honey so that the skin becomes crispy. Scatter the nuts over just before the chicken is ready but do not let them burn.

The chicken and vegetables can be cooked ahead of time and kept in a cold place then reheated with the warmed honey at a later time.

Variation Add one cup bean sprouts to the onions, and before adding the honey, sprinkle with soy sauce, and grill or put into a hot oven.

Israeli Chicken
(chicken cooked with Jaffa oranges)

Ingredients (*serves 4–6*)
1.5–1.75 kg (3–3½ lb) roasting chicken, or equivalent chicken joints, if frozen see they are well thawed
2 tablespoons grated orange rind
450 ml (¾ pint) orange juice
2 heaped tablespoons brown sugar
4 tablespoons melted butter or margarine

2 tablespoons mild French mustard such as Blanc de Dijon
½ teaspoon salt
1 tablespoon cornflour mixed with 2 tablespoons cold water

To garnish
1 large thinly sliced orange

Turn the cooker to HIGH for 20 minutes, at the end of the marinating period (see below). If using a whole chicken, split it in half. Mix together the orange rind, juice, sugar, melted butter, mustard and salt thoroughly. Rub this mixture into the flesh of the chicken, cover and leave for 1 hour.

Put it all carefully into the cooker, cover and cook on LOW for 6–8 hours or on HIGH for 3–4 hours, if using chicken joints, but if a split chicken increase cooking time to 8–10 hours on LOW and 4–5 on HIGH.

If using the removable crockery pot cooker, the dish can be lifted out and put uncovered into a hot oven for the last half an hour's cooking time, to crisp up the skin. But before doing that cream the cornflour with the water and add to the sauce, stirring well. Turn the cooker to HIGH for 20–30 minutes.

Garnish with thinly sliced unpeeled, but pipped orange

Poached Chicken

Ingredients (serves 4–6)

1½–2 kg (3–4 lb) chicken, either a
  boiling bird or roaster (if frozen,
  thaw thoroughly)
1 celery heart, with leaves
1 large leek, or 2 small
1 medium carrot, finely sliced

½ lemon
1 chicken stock cube
salt and freshly ground pepper
1 medium onion, finely sliced
pinch of tarragon and 2 sprigs
  parsley
pinch of mace

Turn the cooker to HIGH for 20 minutes. Then put all ingredients into the cooker, starting with the carrots, leeks, celery and onion. Cover with boiling water. Cook on LOW for 10–12 hours if a boiling bird, or HIGH for 5–6 hours, but if roasting bird then cook for only 7–9 hours on LOW and 3–4 hours on HIGH. If you like dumplings with it, see page 14.

Serve with the sauce of your choice, or use one of the following.

Chicken Liver and Lemon Sauce

Towards the end of cooking time for the poached chicken, make the sauce.

Ingredients

1 or 2 chicken livers
grated rind of 1 lemon and the
  juice
300 ml (½ pint) chicken stock
  (take from the pot)

1 tablespoon flour
1 tablespoon butter or margarine
salt and pepper

Simmer the chicken livers in the stock and when soft, after about

20 minutes, mash them finely in the stock. Add the grated lemon rind and season to taste. Heat the butter in a saucepan and stir in the flour, letting it cook for about 1 minute, add the chicken liver mixture, stirring very well. Let it just bubble up for a minute, and just before serving add the lemon juice.

Tarragon Sauce

Ingredients
2 tablespoons butter or margarine
2 tablespoons flour
generous 300 ml (½ pint) chicken
  stock from the pot

2 teaspoons dried tarragon or 2
  tablespoons chopped fresh
  tarragon
150 ml (¼ pint) cream
salt and pepper

Heat the butter and stir in the flour, letting it cook for 1 minute. Then add the chicken stock, stirring all the time until it is quite smooth. Add the tarragon and season to taste. Finally add the cream, and let it heat up but do not boil.

Paprika Chicken

Paprikahuhn is both a German and Hungarian method of serving chicken in a paprika sauce, which is not hot, but has the characteristically fragrant taste of dried sweet peppers from which paprika is made.
Rabbit can also be cooked this way.

Ingredients (serves 4–6)
1.5–2 kg (3–4 lb) chicken, jointed
  and rolled in seasoned flour (if
  frozen make certain it is well
  thawed)
2 tablespoons oil
1 heaped tablespoon paprika
  powder

1 large onion, sliced
1 litre (1½ pints) chicken stock
1 tablespoon chopped parsley
salt and freshly ground pepper
125 g (4 oz) sliced mushrooms
150 g (5 oz) plain yoghurt or sour
  cream

Turn the cooker to HIGH for 20 minutes. Roll the chicken joints in seasoned flour, heat up the oil and quickly fry them until golden all over. Add the sliced onion and just let it soften but not colour. Sprinkle the paprika over and mix well, then add the stock stirring all the time. When mixed put it all in the cooker, and add half the chopped parsley. Cover and cook at LOW for 6–8 hours, or on HIGH for 3–4 hours. Half an hour before it is ready turn to HIGH and add the finely sliced mushrooms, pushing them under the stock. The mushrooms can be added at the beginning if you wish.

Then 10 minutes before it is ready, stir in the yoghurt or sour cream, put the lid back on and cook at HIGH. Garnish with the remaining parsley.

Sweet-Sour Chicken

Also for turkey joints, pork or rabbit.

Ingredients (serves 6)

6–8 chicken joints, if frozen thaw thoroughly

2 teaspoons paprika

2 tablespoons oil

2 stalks celery, finely chopped

3 tablespoons light brown sugar or honey

2 tablespoons cornflour

½ teaspoon salt

4 tablespoons vinegar

1 tablespoon soy sauce

1 can pineapple (400 g or 14 oz) size

300 ml (½ pint) water, approx. or chicken stock

1 small onion, finely sliced

Turn the cooker to HIGH for 20 minutes. Skin the chicken joints if you prefer and roll them in the paprika, adding a little more if necessary. Heat up the oil and quickly fry them, also just soften the celery. Mix together the sugar or honey, cornflour and salt in a small bowl; then gradually add the pineapple juice, water, vinegar, and soy sauce, mixing very well. Put the sliced onion at the bottom of the cooker, then the chicken joints with the celery and finally the sugar and cornflour mixture, adding a little more water or stock if the chicken is not covered. Cover and cook on LOW for 6–8 hours or on HIGH for 4 hours. Half an hour before the end of the cooking time, add the pineapple cut up very finely and turn the heat to HIGH. Serve with boiled or fried rice or noodles.

Variation 1 small chopped green or red sweet pepper can be added with the onion to make the dish more colourful. Hot bean sprouts go well with it.

Turkish Chicken

Ingredients (serves 6)

6–8 chicken joints, if frozen thaw thoroughly

2 small onions, finely chopped

225 g (8 oz) peeled tomatoes

6 whole black peppercorns

225 g (½ lb) raw rice

1 litre (1½ pints) chicken stock

1 tablespoon chopped fresh herbs, such as parsley, tarragon, chives

50 g (2 oz) blanched almonds

50 g (2 oz) sultanas

salt and pepper

Turn cooker to HIGH for 20 minutes before cooking. Put all the ingredients, except the almonds, into the cooking pot starting with the onions on the bottom, season to taste, then cover and cook on LOW for 6–8 hours, or HIGH for about 4 hours. Check that the rice and chicken are tender, also that the liquid has been absorbed. Just before serving add the blanched almonds, split in half.

Coq au Vin

This is a very good French method of cooking chicken in red wine. Turkey, duck, rabbit and pheasant, not in its first youth, can also be cooked this way.

Ingredients (*serves 6*)
6–8 chicken joints
100 g (4 oz) streaky bacon, cut into cubes
a little seasoned flour
2 medium onions finely chopped
2 chopped garlic cloves

1 bayleaf
bouquet garni of herbs
a bottle of red wine
salt and pepper
100 g (4 oz) mushrooms
8 button onions, blanched
a little oil

To garnish
parsley and croûtons

Turn the cooker to HIGH for 20 minutes. In a frying pan fry the bacon cubes until fairly crisp, then in that fat lightly fry the onions and garlic until soft but not coloured. Put the bayleaf into the bottom of the cooker, add the fried bacon, onions, garlic and bouquet garni on top. Roll the chicken joints in flour, and put on top of the onions. Warm the wine and pour over the chicken. Cook on LOW for about 8 hours, or for 4 hours on HIGH.

One hour before it is ready, heat up some oil and lightly fry the button onions which have been blanched in boiling water for 10 minutes. Add the sliced mushrooms (or whole if they are very small) and let them soften, adding a little more oil if needed. Season to taste.

Just before serving add them to the *coq au vin* and serve with a garnish of chopped parsley and triangular croûtons of fried bread which have been dusted with a little garlic or celery salt.

Chicken Liver Pâté
Other livers can also be used.

Pâté makes very well in the slow cooker, but it is essential to find a tin or heatproof dish which will fit comfortably into the cooker and leave enough space both for the lid to sit properly and for some

43

water to be poured around. Also either a trivet or jam jar lid is needed.

Ingredients (serves up to 12)

1 teaspoon butter
450 g (1 lb) chicken livers
2 tablespoons oil
1 large chopped garlic clove
1 small onion, finely sliced
1 bayleaf

6–8 streaky rashers
2 egg yolks
2–3 tablespoons red wine or brandy
pinch of marjoram
salt and freshly ground pepper

Turn the cooker to HIGH for 20 minutes. Grease the tin for the pâté and line with half the streaky rashers. Heat the oil and quickly brown the livers. Mince or liquidize them with the garlic, onion, marjoram, egg yolks and wine or brandy. Season well, put into the tin and level the top. Then cover with the remaining rashers, put the bayleaf on top and cover with foil.

Stand the tin in the pot on either the trivet or jam jar lid and add enough boiling water to come half-way up the sides. Cook on LOW for 3–4 hours, remove from the pot, but let it cool in the tin, and when cool weigh it.

To serve take out of the tin, by running a hot knife down the sides, chill slightly and serve with hot toast.

Chicken and Liver Paste

This is an old English paste which is delicious.

Ingredients (serves 6–8)

1 lightly cooked, boned chicken, about 1 kg (2½ lb)
225 g (½ lb) chicken livers
225 g (½ lb) bacon
1 chopped shallot or small onion
½ teaspoon lemon thyme or tarragon

1 egg yolk
50 g (2 oz) butter
pinch of ground cloves and allspice
300 ml (½ pint) chicken stock, boiling
salt and freshly ground pepper
100 g (4 oz) approx. melted butter

See recipe above for notes about a suitable tin or dish which will fit into your cooker.

Turn the cooker to HIGH for 20 minutes. Keep the breast separate and slice it. Chop the remaining chicken into small pieces. Mince the liver with the bacon and shallot and mix in the egg yolk and the thyme or tarragon and season. Mix the chopped chicken with the cloves and allspice and season that too.

Grease the tin with the butter. Put a layer of the chopped chicken, then a layer of the liver and bacon mixture, then lay the slices of breast on top. Cover with another layer of liver mixture and finally the chopped chicken. Pour the hot chicken stock over, cover with foil and the lid and cook at HIGH for half an hour, then at LOW for 2–3 hours. Take from the pot, leave to cool, take off the foil and press down with a spoon. When cold cover with the melted butter, and keep cold. Serve cold with a green salad and crusty bread. Leftovers can also be used, but halve the ingredients if they are under the weight given above.

See also *Cock-a-leekie*, page 14, *Duck Korma*, page 47, *Duck with Pineapple* page 49, *Stuffed Turkey Breasts*, page 51.

DUCK

Duck or duckling is often an extravagant bird when roasted, for there is not a lot of flesh on it, and it is quite hard to see that the flesh is not overdone and yet the skin crispy. Cooked in a crock-pot it is much more economical and easier to manage, for the long, slow cooking sees that it is cooked enough, and the subcutaneous fat which can be a problem, melts away into the bottom of the pot.

Baked or Roast Duck

1 If your pot is large enough then leave the bird whole, otherwise cut into portions.

2 Prick it all over with a sharp-pronged fork, so that the fat can drain out.

3 For a roast or baked duck stand on a trivet in the pot, then pour off any excess fat during cooking. This should be done towards the end of cooking time so that the heat balance is not too disturbed.

4 Use the same method and cooking time as for *Baked or Roast Chicken*, page 33, but also follow instructions given above. *If the duck is frozen make certain it is thoroughly thawed.*

Duck Agrodolce

Anitra in Agrodolcè is a famous Roman dish, literally 'duck in sour-sweet', and has been known since earliest times, for the ancient Romans loved the sweet-sour taste, yet it is quite unlike the Chinese one.

Ingredients (serves 4)

1 duck about 1.5 kg (3 lb), cut into portions
2 tablespoons butter or margarine
seasoned flour
2 medium onions, finely sliced
½ teaspoon ground cloves

salt and freshly ground pepper
600 ml (1 pint) giblet stock, or a chicken cube
50 g (2 oz) sugar
2 tablespoons water
2 tablespoons wine vinegar
2 tablespoons fresh mint, chopped

Turn the cooker on to HIGH for 20 minutes. Heat up the butter or margarine until foaming, and roll the duck in seasoned flour. Fry the duck pieces quickly until brown all over, either with or without the skin, but prick skin if leaving on. Remove from the pan, and in the same fat sauté the onions until soft but not coloured, pour off excess fat, shake over the ground cloves and then season. Add the duck, then the giblet stock, let it bubble up, then transfer to the cooker.

Cover, and cook on LOW for 8–10 hours, or HIGH for 4–5 hours.

Towards the end of the cooking time, boil up the sugar with the same amount of water until it becomes light coffee-coloured, then add the wine vinegar. Mix in the fresh chopped mint, stir well, then turn cooker to HIGH and add this to the duck liquid, first checking that there is not an excess of fat on the top. If so, spoon it off before adding the sugar and vinegar mixture.

Duck with Honeyed Apricot Sauce

This is a delicious dish and a change from the more usual duck with orange.

Ingredients (serves 3–4)

1 1.5–2 kg (3–4 lb) duck, either whole or cut into portions

For the sauce

1 large can (900 gr or 30 oz) apricots
2 tablespoons honey

1 tablespoon grated orange peel and the juice
150 ml (¼ pint) dry white wine
1 tablespoon cornflour
1 tablespoon cold water
salt and pepper

Turn the cooker to HIGH for 20 minutes. Prick the skin of the duck all over, then put on a trivet in the cooker, skin side up, season, then mix up sauce ingredients, by first draining the apricots and combining the syrup with the honey, orange peel and juice, the white wine and a little seasoning. Mix well, then brush some of this sauce over the duck or duck portions. Cover and cook on LOW for

8–10 hours. If possible drain off any fat at half cooking time and brush again with the sauce.

Towards end of cooking time, cream the cornflour with the water and mix with the remaining sauce, then heat it up in a saucepan, stirring until it boils and thickens, then add the apricots. Take the duck from the cooker and serve with the sauce over the top.

Variations

1 If using a whole duck, stuff first with cooked rice mixed with a bouquet of chopped herbs and some grated orange peel.

2 Add 1 tablespoon soy sauce to the sauce mixture above, and serve with rice.

3 A little chopped preserved ginger added to the sauce gives a piquant flavour.

Duck with Gooseberry Sauce

Cook the duck as for *Baked Duck*, page 45, but after the fat has been drained off, add 150 ml (¼ pint) red wine. At end of cooking time make the following sauce:

Ingredients (serves 4)

225 g (½ lb) gooseberries
2 tablespoons sugar
1 tablespoon butter

squeeze of lemon
150 ml (¼ pint) dry white wine or cider

Cook the gooseberries with the sugar, white wine and butter until they are puréed. Then liquidize and just before serving add the squeeze of lemon. Serve hot with the duck.

Duck Korma

This is an excellent Indian dish which can also be used for chicken, rabbit, lamb or beef.

Ingredients (serves 4–5)

1 duck 1.5 kg (3–4 lb) cut into portions, and skinned
2 cloves crushed garlic
1 tablespoon ground coriander
1 teaspoon ground cumin
1 teaspoon ground turmeric
pinch of ginger or 1 teaspoon grated green ginger
pinch of saffron (optional)

pinch of cayenne pepper
1 teaspoon salt
300 ml (½ pint) plain yoghurt

For the sauce
2 tablespoons olive oil
1 large onion, thinly sliced
4 cloves
3 cardamom seeds
5 cm (2 in) stick of cinnamon

47

Mix together all the above ingredients except the duck, then add the duck and marinate it in the mixture for at least 1 hour, turning the pieces over so they get covered well. Meanwhile turn the cooker to HIGH and prepare the following: heat 2 tablespoons oil and lightly fry the onion with the cloves, cardamom seeds and the stick of cinnamon. This will only take a few minutes. Remove the cinnamon stick and add the duck pieces and marinade. Let it just heat up, then transfer to the cooker, cover and cook on LOW for 8–10 hours, or 4–5 on HIGH.

Duck with Marsala Wine

Anitra Selvatica is the Italian version of duck with orange, using Marsala wine.

Ingredients (serves 4)

1 1.5–2 kg (3–4 lb) duck, cut into portions
2 tablespoons oil

For the sauce

2 teaspoons olive oil (this gives authentic flavour)

salt and freshly ground pepper
1 clove garlic
1 tablespoon chopped parsley
pinch of sage
5 tablespoons Marsala wine
juice and peel of 1 orange
2–3 tablespoons duck stock (from giblets)

Turn the cooker to HIGH for 20 minutes. Prick the duck all over, then heat up the oil and quickly fry it on all sides. Season well. Take from the oil and put it into the cooker. Make the sauce by heating the oil, parsley, sage and garlic, and when hot add all the other sauce ingredients. Pour half this over the duck, cover and cook on LOW for 8–10 hours and HIGH for 4–5 hours. Half an hour before it is ready, turn the cooker to HIGH and add the rest of the sauce, adding a little more Marsala and stock (about 2 tablespoons mixed) if necessary. Serve with a *Lentil Purée*, see page 111.

Note If cooking both dishes in the crock-pot, then cook the duck the day before and heat up on the stove or in the oven, and cook the lentils the day they are needed in the crock-pot.

Duck with Orange Flambéed with Irish Mist

This is also good for pork.

Ingredients (serves 4)

2 tablespoons oil
flour

1 1.5–2 kg (3–4 lb) duck, either whole or cut into portions
2 tablespoons butter

2 medium onions, finely sliced
grated peel and juice of 2 oranges
6 tablespoons red wine
4 tablespoons stock (made from
  giblets)
salt and pepper

To flambé
4 tablespoons warmed Irish Mist,
  which is an Irish liqueur made
  from whiskey, honey and herbs

Turn the cooker to HIGH for 20 minutes. Heat up the oil in a frying pan, then rub the duck or portions in seasoned flour and brown quickly on all sides. Remove from the oil and put into the cooker.

Heat up the butter until foaming, fry the onions until they are soft but not coloured, then add all the other ingredients, except the Irish Mist. Cover and cook on LOW for 8–10 hours, or HIGH for 4–5 hours. Before serving, warm up the Irish Mist by holding it in a ladle over a flame, then pour over the duck and set fire to it. Serve at once, or preferably flambé it at the table.

Duck with Pineapple
Po Lo Chiang is a marvellous Chinese method.

Ingredients (serves 6)
1 1.5–2 kg (3–4 lb) duck, whole or
  cut into serving portions
salt and pepper

For the garnish
1 small can (200 g or 7 oz) drained
  pineapple
4 pieces preserved ginger, in syrup

For the sauce
300 ml (½ pint) pineapple juice
4 tablespoons syrup from the ginger
  (or use liquid honey and ground
  ginger, mixed)
2 teaspoons cornflour
3 tablespoons sherry
1 teaspoon soy sauce

Turn the cooker to HIGH for 20 minutes. Prick the duck and rub all over with salt and pepper, then put it on to a trivet in the cooker, add 150 ml (¼ pint) of boiling water, cover and cook for 8–10 hours on LOW or 4–5 on HIGH.

Meanwhile make the sauce, by heating the pineapple juice with the ginger syrup. Cream the cornflour and add to the pineapple and ginger, stirring and heating until it thickens slightly and is smooth. Then add the sherry and soy sauce, and keep warm.

Remove the duck from the cooker, and let it cool a little, then remove the bones. Heat it through in the duck stock at the bottom of the cooker before putting it on to a warm serving dish and garnish it with alternate pieces of chopped pineapple and chopped preserved ginger. Pour the sauce over all and serve on a bed of boiled rice.

Duck with Port

This is also good for wild duck, teal or widgeon; they will take 1 hour less cooking time as they are smaller birds.

Ingredients (serves 4–6)

1 1.5–2 kg (3–4 lb) duck, whole or jointed
juice of 1 lemon
salt and pepper
225 g (½ lb) mushrooms

4 tablespoons oil

For the sauce

300 ml (½ pint) port
1 teaspoon mushroom ketchup
4 tablespoons brandy, warmed

Turn the cooker to HIGH for 20 minutes. Rub the bird, which has been pricked all over with a fork, with salt and pepper and sprinkle over about half the lemon juice. Put on top of a trivet in the cooker, cover and cook on LOW for 8–10 hours or 4–5 on HIGH. As the end of cooking time approaches, slice the mushrooms and soften them in the hot oil; do not let them crisp up. Then warm the port and mushroom ketchup and add the mushrooms (without any oil). Do not let it boil for longer than 1 minute. Put the duck on to the warmed serving dish, pour over the port and mushrooms, then warm the brandy in a ladle, pour over and ignite. Serve at once.

Duck au Vin

See *Coq au Vin*, page 43, but remember to prick the skin of the duck first. Many of the chicken recipes are suitable for duck, so consult index for other methods.

Duck Pâté

See *Chicken and Liver Paste*, page 44, *Hare Pâté*, page 59, also *Game Pâté*, page 60, and *Turkey with Cherries*, page 52.

Guinea Fowl

Guinea fowl is not often seen these days, but it is a very good little bird, not unlike a pheasant and usually cheaper. It can be cooked as pheasant, and the following West Country method (where it is known as Gliny) is very good.

Roast and Stuffed Guinea Fowl

The birds usually weigh about 1 kg (2¼ lb).

Ingredients (serves 2–3)

1 guinea fowl
3 bacon rashers, chopped

225 g (½ lb) sausagemeat
chopped liver of the bird
a pinch of mixed spice and nutmeg

300 ml (½ pint) stock, either from giblets or a dissolved chicken cube

salt and pepper
6 tablespoons port or cider
3 tablespoons double cream

Turn the cooker to HIGH for 20 minutes. Mix together the sausagemeat, chopped liver, nutmeg and mixed spice and stuff the bird with it. Heat up the chopped bacon rashers and quickly fry the bird in the fat when it runs out. Put into the cooker with the bacon (not the fat), the stock and the port, and season to taste.

Cover and cook on LOW for 7 hours, or on HIGH for 3½ hours. Ten minutes before it is ready, turn to HIGH and taste for seasoning, then add the cream, cover and heat it up for not longer than the 10 minutes.

Serve with redcurrant jelly.

TURKEY

Obviously a whole turkey won't fit into your crock-pot, but this form of cooking is very good for turkey joints or breasts which are sold separately, and it is also useful for getting the most out of leftover turkey. It is especially useful at Christmas time when one has had enough of cooking by the time the leftovers are reached, and they can be put in the crock-pot with rice or a sauce, either home-made or canned, and conveniently forgotten until wanted.

Many of the chicken recipes can be used for turkey joints, so check in the index.

Note If using frozen turkey portions make quite certain they are thawed before starting to cook.

Turkey Breasts, Stuffed, Cordon Bleu
This is also excellent for chicken breasts.

Ingredients (serves 2)
2 whole turkey breasts, skinned and boned
4 slices of cooked ham, about 10 cm (4 in) long and 5 cm (2 in) wide
4 pieces Gruyère cheese the same size as ham

2 tablespoons flour mixed with 2 tablespoons grated Parmesan cheese
salt and freshly ground pepper
3–4 tablespoons oil
150 ml (¼ pint) dry white wine

Turn the cooker to HIGH for 20 minutes. Cut each turkey breast in half, then put between greaseproof paper or thin plastic and pound until thin. Remove from paper and spread first the ham, then the cheese on the turkey breast, then roll up and tuck the ends in like a parcel. If necessary secure each with a small skewer or cocktail stick. Mix together the flour, Parmesan cheese, salt and pepper, then roll the turkey breasts in the mixture until they are quite thickly coated. Put into the refrigerator for about an hour.

Heat up the oil in a frying pan and sauté the stuffed breasts on all sides quickly. Place in the cooker, pour the wine carefully around, cover and cook on LOW for 4–6 hours or on HIGH for 2–3 hours. *Variation* Use a breadcrumb and herb stuffing.

Turkey Casserole
This is an Italian dish called *Tacchino Stufato*.

Ingredients (*serves 4*)
4 legs or legs and wings of turkey
3 tablespoons flour
3–4 tablespoons oil
8 small onions, finely sliced
100 g (4 oz) mushrooms, sliced
1 teaspoon basil, chopped

2 cloves chopped garlic
½ lemon, sliced
300 ml (½ pint) turkey stock or chicken stock
150 ml (¼ pint) white wine
salt
freshly ground pepper

Turn the cooker to HIGH for 20 minutes. Roll the turkey joints in seasoned flour. Heat up the oil and quickly brown them in it, before transferring them to the slow cooker. Sauté the onions in the oil until soft and mix them with the turkey. Add a little more oil if needed and soften the mushrooms, adding the garlic, basil and lemon slices. Season, pour in the turkey stock, and when it simmers, add the wine. Taste for seasoning, then pour over the turkey and onion in the cooker, cover and cook on LOW for 8–10 hours or on HIGH for 4–5 hours.

Variation Add some finely sliced celery and green or red sweet peppers, and when in season some sliced chestnuts are extremely good.

Turkey with Cherries
This is also very good with duck.

Ingredients (*serves 3–4*)
the breasts of the bird, sliced and rolled in seasoned flour
2 tablespoons oil or butter

6 tablespoons Madeira wine
salt and freshly ground pepper
900 g (2 lb) canned black cherries
1 teaspoon red wine vinegar

Turn the cooker to HIGH for 20 minutes. Slice the turkey breasts and flatten them slightly, then roll in seasoned flour. Heat the oil or butter and lightly sauté them before adding the Madeira and seasoning. Add half the cherries and all the juice, put into the cooker, cover and cook on LOW for 6–8 hours or HIGH for 3–4 hours. Just before it is ready, liquidize the remaining cherries with the vinegar and heat through. Serve this sauce poured over the turkey.

Turkey with Cranberries and Honey

Ingredients (serves 2–4)
2–4 turkey thighs
seasoned flour
2 tablespoons oil
salt and pepper

225 g (½ lb) cranberries
225 g (½ lb) liquid honey
300 ml (½ pint) turkey or chicken
   stock

Turn the cooker to HIGH for 20 minutes. Remove the skin from the turkey thighs, then roll in seasoned flour. Heat up the oil and quickly brown them on all sides. Put into the cooker with the cranberries, cover with the honey and chicken stock which should be brought to boiling point. Season, cover and cook on LOW for 6–8 hours, or on HIGH for 3–4 hours.

Turkey with Marsala

See *Duck with Marsala*, page 48, and the most suitable parts of the bird to use are either the breast or the thighs.

Turkey Risotto

This is excellent for Christmas leftovers.

Ingredients (serves 4–5)
675–900 g (1½–2 lb) turkey meat
   leftovers, according to size of pot
1 medium onion, finely sliced
1 medium red, or green pepper,
   sliced
100–175 g (4–6 oz) sliced
   mushrooms
salt and freshly ground pepper
175–224 g (6–8 oz) long grain rice
½ teaspoon tarragon

6 peeled and sliced tomatoes or
   equivalent can
600 ml (1 pint) stock for 175 g
   (6 oz) rice, increasing to 900 ml
   (1½ pints) for 225 g (8 oz)
4 tablespoons white wine

To garnish
sliced black olives and chopped
   parsley

Turn the cooker to HIGH for 20 minutes. Put all the ingredients into the pot, cover and cook on LOW for 6–8 hours or HIGH for 3–4 hours. Garnish with sliced black olives and plenty of chopped parsley, and serve with a salad.

Turkey Terrine

Double the quantities can be made if crock-pot is large enough but do not increase soup measure.

Ingredients (serves 4–6)
450 g (1 lb) raw, minced turkey meat
100 g (4 oz) fresh breadcrumbs
1 tablespoon rolled oats

1 small chopped onion or garlic clove
½ can condensed mushroom soup
1 beaten egg
salt and freshly ground pepper

Before starting to cook find a suitable sized dish to fit in the cooker, or you can put the terrine directly into the dish.

Turn the cooker to HIGH for 20 minutes. Mix all ingredients together, adding the egg last. Put into the container or crock-pot, cover and cook on LOW for 5–6 hours. The terrine can be served hot with cranberry sauce, or taken out, chilled and served in slices with hot toast.

See also *Chicken and Liver Paste*, page 44, *Sweet-Sour Chicken*, page 42, and *Coq au Vin*, page 43.

GAME

There are two kinds of game: furred and feathered. The latter, except for pigeon, is nowadays quite expensive and therefore often roasted. However, the slow cooking method is excellent for it does not shrink the bird in cooking. Also because second-year birds, which can be tough if roasted, have time to tenderize in the slow cooking method. Often these older birds are quite cheap and make the most delicious casseroles, pâtés and terrines.

Braised Game Birds

This recipe comes from the Lake Vyrnwy Hotel, Oswestry, Shropshire on the Welsh border, and can be used for any elderly game birds or a mixture.

Ingredients (serves 8)
2 onions, finely sliced
1 carrot, finely sliced
2 celery stalks, finely sliced
game giblets
4 whole allspice berries
bouquet garni of herbs
1 bayleaf

water
4 game birds cut in half
3 tablespoons oil
1 medium can consommé
4–6 tablespoons red wine
salt and freshly ground pepper
1 tablespoon flour

Turn the cooker to HIGH for 20 minutes. Prepare all the vegetables and put with the giblets into the cooker with the herbs, season to taste, barely cover with water and cook on HIGH. Meanwhile heat up the oil and quickly fry the birds on all sides for 3–4 minutes. Then put them on top of the vegetables in the crock pot, add the consommé and wine and season again. Cover and cook on LOW for 8–10 hours, or HIGH for 4–5 hours. Just before it is ready, mix the flour with a little stock, turn to HIGH and stir this in, then continue cooking for half an hour.

Game Braised with Grapes

Grouse, partridge, pigeon or pheasant can be used.

Ingredients (serves 2–4)

2 game birds, cut in half (more birds can be used if size of cooker allows)

4 rashers bacon

150 ml ($\frac{1}{4}$ pint) dry white wine

225 g ($\frac{1}{2}$ lb) seeded, peeled white grapes

salt and freshly ground white pepper

Turn the cooker to HIGH for 20 minutes. Wrap each half of the birds in the bacon, then heat up a frying pan and quickly turn them so that the bacon is slightly browned and the fat has run out. Put them into the cooker, season and add half the grapes and the wine. Cover and cook on LOW for 8–10 hours. Half an hour before serving add the rest of the grapes.

Partridge au Vin

See *Coq au Vin*, page 43, but only use enough wine to barely cover the bird.

Partridge with Cabbage

If the partridges are very old, then cook them for 2 hours at HIGH before adding the cabbage.

Ingredients (serves about 4)

2 partridges cut in half

4 rashers bacon

1 medium to large white cabbage

salt and freshly ground pepper

1 medium can consommé

water

3 tablespoons dry sherry

Turn the cooker to HIGH for 20 minutes. Season the birds well and wrap them in the bacon. Trim the cabbage and take off four large outer leaves which are not discoloured. Remove the stalks and blanch them in boiling water for 1 minute. Take out, pat dry and wrap each bacon-covered half bird in one of the leaves, tucking in the ends like a parcel. Shred the rest of the cabbage fairly coarsely, put half into the cooker, season, lay the birds on top, then cover with the rest of the cabbage and season again. Pour over the consommé, made up to 600 ml (1 pint) with water. Cover and cook at LOW for 8 hours, or on HIGH for 4 hours. Half an hour before it is ready, taste for seasoning, add the sherry and mix well, and continue cooking on HIGH.

Partridge with Red Cabbage and Cider
Also for pigeon, pheasant, hare or rabbit.

Ingredients (*serves 4*)
2 partridges, cut in half
4 rashers bacon
1 small sliced onion
1 medium-size red cabbage, finely
  sliced

600 ml (1 pint) cider
12 cooked chestnuts (optional)
1 teaspoon vinegar
salt and pepper

Turn the cooker to HIGH for 20 minutes. Wrap the partridges, which have been cut in half, in the bacon rashers and fry them quickly in a hot pan, so that the bacon browns slightly. Mix the red cabbage with the sliced onion and put into the cooker. Season well and pour over the cider and vinegar. Then put the birds on top, cover and cook on LOW for 8–10 hours, or on HIGH for 4–5 hours. Half an hour before serving add the chestnuts, cut in half if they are large.

Pheasant with Apple and Onion Purée
Also for pigeon.

Ingredients (*serves about 3*)
1 well-hung pheasant
2–3 bacon rashers
450 g (1 lb) apples
450 g (1 lb) onions
salt and pepper

3 tablespoons oil
a pinch of cinnamon
150 ml ($\frac{1}{4}$ pint) bianco vermouth or
  sweet white wine
4 tablespoons dry white wine

Turn the cooker to HIGH for 20 minutes. The pheasants can be left whole or cut into serving joints, whichever is most convenient, and wrapped in the bacon rashers. Prepare the apples and onions, by peeling, coring the apples, then slicing very finely. Heat up the oil and lightly fry them until soft but not coloured. Add the cinnamon, seasoning, and the vermouth, mixing well. Put this into the cooker and the bird on top; pour over the white wine. Cover and cook on LOW for 8–10 hours, or on HIGH for 4–5 hours.

Take out the pheasant and put on to a warmed serving dish. Put the apple and onion purée around and serve.

Pheasant Casserole
Partridge or pigeon can also be used.

Ingredients (serves 3)
1 well-hung pheasant
2–3 tablespoons oil
1 celery heart, chopped finely
1 medium onion, finely sliced
grated rind and juice of 1 lemon
1 medium can consommé
bouquet of herbs
2 tablespoons medium sherry
salt and freshly ground pepper

Turn the cooker to HIGH for 20 minutes. Wipe the pheasant all over and squeeze a little lemon juice inside. Heat up the oil and brown it on all sides. Take out and soften the onion and celery in the same oil, but do not let them colour. Season before putting them into the cooker. Place the pheasant on top. Heat up the consommé, with lemon juice and sherry. Put the herbs and grated lemon rind into the liquid and pour over the bird.

Check the seasoning. Cover and cook on HIGH for 20 minutes, then on LOW for 8–10 hours or HIGH for 4–5 hours.

Variation Use red wine instead of the sherry and garnish with lightly fried mushrooms.

See also *Braised Game Birds*, page 54 and *Game Braised with Grapes*, page 55. Some of the chicken recipes are also suitable for game birds, so consult the index.

Pigeon Casserole

Ingredients (serves 4)
4 pigeons
1 packet sage and onion stuffing
2–3 tablespoons cooking oil
1 medium onion, finely sliced
1 celery heart, finely sliced
flour
600 ml (1 pint) chicken stock or cider
salt and pepper

Turn the cooker to HIGH for 20 minutes. Wipe the pigeons inside and out, then make up the stuffing. Heat the oil and quickly brown the pigeons all over. Allow to cool slightly before stuffing them. In the same oil soften the onion and celery, add a sprinkling of flour, mix well and season. Pour in the stock and mix over heat until it thickens. Put into the cooker, lay the birds on top, cover and cook on HIGH for 20 minutes, then LOW for 7–8 hours.

Pigeons Stuffed with Almonds, Apricots and Raisins

Ingredients (serves 4)
4 pigeons

For the stuffing
1 medium onion, sliced
2 tablespoons oil
2 tablespoons raisins

1 tablespoon chopped parsley
grated rind and juice of ½ lemon
2 tablespoons cooked, chopped dried apricots, or canned
2 tablespoons blanched, split almonds

Turn the cooker to HIGH for 20 minutes. Slice the onion, heat the oil and soften the onion in it. Then add the raisins and almonds and fry for a minute or two. Put into a bowl and add all the other ingredients, mix well and stuff the birds with this mixture. The cooking time is the same as for recipe above (*Pigeon Casserole*).

Variation Stuff the birds with soaked, chopped prunes mixed with peeled chopped apple, and use dark beer instead of the stock or cider.

FURRED GAME

All furred game (and also pigeon) tastes better if it is marinated before cooking. The marinade can be quite simple, such as red or white wine, cider, a little oil, a sliced onion, sliced carrot, a bayleaf, rosemary, salt and pepper. Two tablespoons of oil are enough for 300 ml (½ pint) of wine or cider. Some is used in the cooking, and the rest can be frozen for future use.

The marinade should come to at least half-way up the game, and the joints turned frequently so that all sides are soaked in it. Game can be left for one to two days in a marinade, and for not less than overnight. Dry the joints before sautéeing.

HARE

A hare is often too large for a small family, but it is good value. If the hare is young, then cut off the legs and use them for jugging, pâté, or a casserole; roast the saddle. The bones make a good soup with onions, celery, carrot, etc.
It is wise to marinate hare for at least 24 hours before cooking.

Jugged Hare

Ingredients (serves 4–6)
1 hare, jointed, or use the legs

marinade, as above, using 300 ml (½ pint)

2 tablespoons oil
1 tablespoon flour
3 cloves garlic, chopped
3 medium onions, chopped
2 carrots, finely sliced
2 celery stalks, chopped

1 teaspoon powdered oregano
pinch of mace or nutmeg
1 tablespoon redcurrant jelly
300 ml ($\frac{1}{2}$ pint) red wine or port
grated rind and juice of $\frac{1}{2}$ lemon
salt and freshly ground pepper

Marinate the hare overnight if possible. Then turn the cooker to HIGH when you are preparing the hare, for about 20 minutes. Take the joints from the marinade, pat them dry, heat up the oil and fry them all over. Set aside and in the same oil soften the onions, garlic, carrots and celery, shake over the flour, season, and add the marinade. Pour into the cooker, add the herbs and spices, the hare, and finally the grated rind and juice of the lemon, the redcurrant jelly and the wine. Season again to taste, then cover and cook on LOW for 10–12 hours, or on HIGH for 6 hours.

If you have the blood of the hare, you can mix it with 1 tablespoon redcurrant jelly and 1 tablespoon of cream. Turn the cooker to HIGH for the last half hour and add this, stirring well.

Hare Pâté

This can be made from any part of the hare, either raw or cooked. If using uncooked meat, first marinate it overnight, in the marinade given on page 58. The pâté can be made in the cooker or in a suitable container which will fit easily into the cooker.

Ingredients (serves 8–10)
450 g (1 lb) hare meat, minced
450 g (1 lb) minced pork or veal
2 tablespoons sherry or brandy
2 bayleaves
2 cloves garlic, chopped

2 egg yolks
4 tablespoons hare stock or
  marinade
salt and freshly ground pepper
a little butter or margarine

Turn the cooker to HIGH for 20 minutes. Mix together the hare meat, hare stock or marinade, garlic and 1 egg yolk and season well. Mix the pork or veal with the other egg yolk, the sherry or brandy and seasonings. Grease the cooker or container well. Put a bayleaf on the bottom, followed by a layer of minced hare, then veal or pork and so on until all the meat is finished, ending with a layer of hare. Put the other bayleaf on top, cover with foil, then add boiling water to half-way up the sides. Put the lid on and cook at LOW for 6–8 hours, or HIGH for 3–4 hours. Leave to cool before taking out of the cooker, cover with a fresh piece of foil and weight it until it is quite cold. Serve cut into slices with hot toast.

This pâté can be made with a mixture of game, such as rabbit, pheasant, venison, etc. See also *Rabbit with Beer and Prunes*.

Rabbit with Beer and Prunes
Also for hare.

This is an excellent method for cooking rabbit, which makes it taste almost like pheasant.

Ingredients (serves 3–4)
1 jointed rabbit
seasoned flour
2–3 tablespoons oil
2 large onions, finely sliced
600 ml (1 pint) dark beer, or $\frac{1}{2}$ Guinness and $\frac{1}{2}$ water
pinch of powdered oregano
salt and pepper
175 g (6 oz) soaked prunes

Turn the cooker to HIGH for 20 minutes. Roll the rabbit joints in seasoned flour. Heat up the oil and lightly fry them. Set aside and in the same oil (adding a little more if needed) just soften the onions, and mix in the oregano. Put the rabbit back, season, and add the beer and the drained prunes. Let it bubble up before transferring to the cooker. Cover and cook on LOW for 6–8 hours, or HIGH for 3–4 hours.

Normandy Rabbit

Ingredients (serves 3–4)
1 rabbit, jointed
seasoned flour
2–3 tablespoons oil or butter
1 medium onion, finely sliced
2 tablespoons chopped parsley
1 can tomatoes, 210 g (7$\frac{1}{2}$ oz)
2 tablespoons tomato purée
pinch mixed herbs, fresh if possible
300 ml ($\frac{1}{2}$ pint) cider
salt and pepper

Turn the cooker to HIGH for 20 minutes. Roll the rabbit joints in seasoned flour. Heat up the oil and quickly fry them all over. Push aside, and fry the onion until soft but not coloured. Add the tomato purée, the tomatoes, herbs and the cider. Let it all bubble up, then season and transfer to the cooker. Cover and cook on HIGH for 20 minutes, then on LOW for 6–8 hours, or on HIGH for 3–4 hours. Serve thickly garnished with chopped parsley.

Spicy Honey Glazed Rabbit
Chicken is also very good done this way.

Ingredients (serves 3–4)
1 jointed rabbit, coated with flour
100 g (4 oz) butter
6 tablespoons honey
300 ml (½ pint) chicken stock
2 tablespoons Blanc de Dijon
  mustard
2 level teaspoons curry powder
salt
parsley for garnishing

Turn the cooker to HIGH for 20 minutes. Meanwhile, cream the butter, and mix thoroughly with the honey, mustard and curry powder; coat the floured rabbit joints with this. Put into the cooker, then pour in the warmed chicken stock. Cover and cook on LOW for 6–8 hours and on HIGH for 3–4 hours. Baste with the honey stock before serving and garnish with parsley.

Many of the chicken recipes are suitable for rabbit. See *Chicken Cacciatora* page 34, *Country Chicken Casserole*, page 36, *Chicken Curry*, page 37, *Paprika Chicken*, page 41, *Sweet-sour Chicken*, page 42, and *Turkish Chicken*, page 42. Also *Coq au Vin*, page 43, *Hare Pâté*, page 59, *Chicken and Liver Paste*, page 44, and *Duck Korma*, page 47.

VENISON

Venison cooks very well in the crock-pot. Any recipe for *Beef*, pages 63–81, can be used for venison, also *Jugged Hare*, page 58, can be adapted to venison, and it should always be marinated first, in the marinade given on page 58. See also *Game Pâté*, page 60.

Meat

All meats are good cooked in the slow cooker, even the cheapest cuts are tenderized and there is little shrinkage. The slow cooker is not just for braising joints or pieces of meat, for it also roasts very well. But do remember that the root vegetables will take as long, if not longer to cook than the meat so see that they are finely sliced or chopped and put at the bottom of the cooker, or around the sides, and see that they are covered by liquid.

It is not necessary to brown the meat first for casseroles, etc. as all the juices will go into the pot, but if the meat is a bit fatty, browning in a frying pan means that you can pour off the excess fat before putting it into the slow cooker. If you like a little fat then stand the joint on a small rack or trivet, so that the fat drips underneath. Follow these instructions and you will have perfectly cooked meat.

1 Make quite certain that the meat is thoroughly thawed, and at room temperature before cooking.

2 Different pieces of meat cook differently: the thickness, the amount of fat and bone and the quality all change the cooking time, so cook until the minimum time given, then test for tenderness. If you are out all day, even if it is done at the minimum time, the extra hour of slow cooking won't harm it, or cause the dish to run dry.

3 Each variety of cooker is slightly different in performance, so when cooking any recipe, check with your own booklet for cooking times.

Directions for Roasting all Meats

1 Check with the size of your cooker as to the shape and weight of joint you will buy. The lid must sit properly over the meat.
The 3–4 litre (5–6 pint) cooker will take a 2–2.5 kg (4–5 lb) joint, whereas the smaller models 2 litre (3¼ pint) will take up to 1.5 kg (3 lb).

2 Dry and season the meat well, then brown in a frying pan in a little oil or fat.

3 Preheat the cooker on HIGH for 20 minutes before putting the joint in, and when browned put into the cooker, on a rack or trivet if it is fatty.

Note For models with the lift-out stoneware pot, roast on HIGH all the time. Please consult your booklet before cooking.

Pork The rind should be cut off before cooking and pre-frying, and the cooker should be on HIGH all the time. A 1–1.75 kg (2–3½ lb) joint takes 3–5 hours and 1.75–2.5 kg (3½–5 lb) takes 4–6 hours.

Beef * All your favourite casserole or braising recipes can be used in the slow cooker, but here are some which might be new to you.

Boeuf à la Mode

This famous dish is delicious cold, when it will be a jelly, and served with freshly-cooked carrots set in the jelly, along with a jacket-baked potato. Lamb is good done in this way, too.

Ingredients (serves 6–8)
1.5–2 kg (3–4 lb) lean beef
2–3 tablespoons oil
1 pig's trotter, split
1 medium can consommé
4 tablespoons warmed brandy
150 ml (¼ pint) red or white wine
1 clove garlic, chopped
bouquet garni of herbs
2–3 shallots or small onions, finely sliced
salt and freshly ground pepper
450 g (1 lb) carrots

Turn the cooker to HIGH for 20 minutes. The beef should be lean rump, or topside, trimmed of fat, but if possible larded through the flesh with strips of pork fat. Many good butchers will do this for you, but strips of fat threaded through a larding needle can be done at home. The needle, threaded with the fat, is drawn through the joints at about 5 cm (2 in) intervals. But it still makes an excellent dish without larding.

Heat up the oil, brown the joint on all sides and just soften the onions. Season well and pour over the warm brandy and ignite. When the flames have died down add the consommé, the wine, herbs and garlic and split pig's foot. Transfer to the cooker, cover and cook on HIGH for 30 minutes, then on LOW for 10–12 hours.

When cooked, take out the meat and let it get cold. Meanwhile strain the stock and when it is quite cold remove any fat from the

* For beef, lamb and veal cook on HIGH for 30 minutes, then for a 1–1.75 kg (2–3½ lb) joint cook on LOW for 4–6 hours and for a 1.75–2.5 (3½–5 lb) joint cook on LOW for 5–7 hours.

top, and taste for seasoning. Then cook the carrots and slice them thinly.

To serve cold, carve the beef into thin slices and either reconstitute, or place the slices in a deep dish, overlapping and interspersed with sliced carrots. Heat the jelly until it is just pourable but not too hot. Pour over and chill the dish. Serve with salad and jacket-baked potatoes.

See also *Boeuf en Daube*, page 67.

Boeuf Bourguignonne

This is the famous beef casserole from Burgundy. Any of the lean cuts of stewing beef can be used, but all are better if first marinated overnight in red wine and oil with herbs, etc. See *Game*, page 58.

Ingredients (serves 4–6)
2 tablespoons oil
1 kg (2¼ lb) stewing steak, cut into cubes
100 g (4 oz) bacon
2 level tablespoons flour

For the garnish
12 button onions
12 button mushrooms

a squeeze of lemon and a nut of butter
½ bottle red wine or ¼ bottle wine and 150 ml (¼ pint) marinade
2 tablespoons brandy (optional)
pinch of oregano
a bayleaf
2 crushed garlic cloves
salt and pepper

Turn the cooker to HIGH for 20 minutes. If the meat has been marinated, drain and reserve the marinade. Wipe the beef dry, heat up the oil, and put in the chopped bacon which has been blanched in boiling water for 2 minutes. When the fat has run out, brown the beef quickly over a high flame. Shake over the flour and mix well, then add the wine, and when warm pour over the brandy and ignite. Add the remaining ingredients and season well. Bring to the boil, then transfer to the cooker. Cook on HIGH for 20 minutes, then switch to LOW for 6–8 hours.

One hour before it is ready, blanch the onions and mushrooms in boiling water which has had a squeeze of lemon added and a nut of butter. Cover with foil and leave to cook for 7–10 minutes. Add these to the beef, turning the cooker to HIGH for at least half an hour.

Croûtons of bread (sliced, cut in half in triangles) then fried quickly in oil, are good with this dish, or alternately thick slices of crusty French bread go well. Fresh root vegetables such as carrots can also accompany the beef.

Beef with Beans

This makes a very good and satisfying meal using very little meat. Lamb or pork can also be used.

Ingredients (serves 6–8)

450 g (1 lb) red kidney beans, soaked

450 g (1 lb) trimmed stewing beef, cubed

2 bacon rashers, chopped

½ teaspoon ground marjoram

1 level teaspoon ground cumin

salt and pepper

200 g (7 oz) canned tomatoes

2 garlic cloves

1 medium onion

2 celery stalks

1.8 litres (3 pints) half water and half beef stock

Note If using the 1.75 litre (3¼ pint) crock-pot, halve the ingredients, and pre-cook the beans on LOW overnight with water to cover.

Turn the cooker to HIGH for 20 minutes. The beans must be soaked overnight in cold water and drained before cooking. Put all ingredients into the cooker, seeing that the vegetables are finely chopped and the meat trimmed and cubed. Stir well so all ingredients are thoroughly mixed. Cover and cook on LOW for 8–10 hours, or on HIGH for 4–6 hours.

Quick Method Cook the vegetables, herbs and beef with 600 ml (1 pint) stock on LOW for about 6 hours, then test for tenderness. Add 2 cans (425 g or 15 oz) drained red kidney beans, mix in well with the meat and vegetables, and turn cooker to HIGH for 20–30 minutes, or until beans are hot through.

Variation Use cubed lamb, pork or veal, or a mixture. Frankfurter sausages can also be used.

Boeuf Carbonnade Flamande

This is a good Flemish dish cooked with beer.

Ingredients (serves 4–6)

1 kg (2¼ lb) lean stewing steak

2–3 tablespoons oil

4 medium onions, finely sliced

300 ml (½ pint) draught bitter beer

300 ml (½ pint) beef stock

2 bayleaves

2 level tablespoons flour

salt and pepper

1 level tablespoon brown sugar

bouquet garni

1 teaspoon French mustard

1 tablespoon wine vinegar

To garnish

4–6 slices of bread toasted on one side only, the untoasted side spread with Blanc de Dijon mustard

Turn the cooker to HIGH for 20 minutes. Trim the meat and cut into cubes. Heat the oil and quickly fry the meat until brown. Then push aside or remove and soften the sliced onions in the same oil. Add the bayleaves, sprinkle over the flour and pour in the beer and stock. Season to taste then add all remaining ingredients except the vinegar. Bring to the boil and transfer to the cooker. Cover and cook on LOW for 6–8 hours, or on HIGH for 3–4 hours. Half an hour before it is ready add the vinegar and stir well. Just before serving put in the bread slices, cut in half, mustard side down on top of the carbonnade.

Beef Curry

Use recipe for *Chicken Curry*, page 37, substituting 1 kg (2¼ lb) beef for the chicken. It is not necessary to fry the meat first.

Boiled Corned Beef and Dumplings

Ingredients (serves 6–8)
1.5–2 kg (3–4 lb) salted
  brisket or silverside
1 medium onion, sliced
1 teaspoon mustard powder
2 sprigs parsley
boiling water

Dumplings (or see *Dumplings*,
  page 14)
100 g (4 oz) self-raising flour
50 g (2 oz) suet or margarine
salt and pepper
water to mix

Soak the meat overnight in water, then drain. Turn the cooker to HIGH for 20 minutes, then put all ingredients into the pot, barely covering the meat with boiling water. Cover and cook on LOW for 10–12 hours, or on HIGH for 5–6 hours. Half an hour before making the dumplings turn the cooker to HIGH. Mix the flour and suet with salt and add just enough water to make a firm, yet elastic dough. Divide into about 6–8 small balls, drop into the crock-pot, cover and continue cooking on HIGH for about 30 minutes.

Instead of dumplings you can use a small cabbage cut into little wedges and add it to the pot about half-way through cooking time.

Glazed Corned Beef
Also for boiled bacon or ham.

Cook as for *Boiled Corned Beef*, above, and when cooked lift th

meat from the pot and put it into a roasting tin. Mix together
2 tablespoons brown sugar, 1 tablespoon black treacle, 2 level
tablespoons French mustard, 1 tablespoon horseradish and 1
tablespoon red wine vinegar. Brush this all over the meat and put
into a hot oven (200°C, 400°F, gas 6) for about 20 minutes, brushing
with the glaze twice during cooking.

The stock: taste the stock for saltiness, and if it is not too salty,
then use it to make *Split Pea Soup*, page 18.

Boeuf en Daube

To serve 8–10

This is similar to *Boeuf à la Mode*, and the word *Daube* comes from
the dish it was originally cooked in, a *daubière*. It is delicious.

Follow the recipe for *Boeuf à la Mode* (page 63), but before cooking
the meat, slice it thinly and cover each slice with minced ham
(approximately 175 g or 6 oz) or very thin slices of ham, mixed with
a few fresh, chopped herbs. When all slices are used, reconstitute
the joint and tie it up, before sautéeing in oil. When cooked, put
the joint into a deep dish and pour over the strained and defatted
stock. Chill and serve cold with string removed. It should be cut
downwards, so that each slice is marbled with the ham, sandwich
fashion.

Stuffed Beef Flank

This is a lean and reasonably priced cut of beef which can be
cooked in many ways. It is ideal for the slow cooking method and
can be served hot or cold.

Ingredients (serves 4–6)
1 kg (2¼ lb) beef flank
350 g (12 oz) sausagemeat
2 bayleaves
1 teaspoon black peppercorns,
  whole

pinch of ground marjoram
salt
300 ml (½ pint) beef stock, or
  consommé

Turn the cooker to HIGH for 20 minutes. Trim off any skin or fat
from the flank, and lightly score one side with a sharp knife but do
not cut through the meat. Put 1 bayleaf on top of the scored side.
Mix together the sausagemeat, peppercorns, marjoram and salt, and
spoon this mixture on to the steak, either rolling up or folding the
sides and ends in securely. Skewer together, or tie with cotton twine.

Stand on a small rack, trivet, or jam jar lid in the cooker, pour over the beef stock, cover and cook on LOW for 8–10 hours, or until the meat is tender when pricked with a fork.

If serving cold, take out and, when cool, wrap in foil, then weight it, and when quite cold, cut into thin slices and serve with a Sauce Vinaigrette, made from 3 parts of oil to 1 of wine vinegar, with 1 tablespoon of chopped herbs and the same of chopped capers in it.

Variations

1 Stuff with a package of breadcrumb and herb stuffing, and after 8 hours' cooking add 225 g (½ lb) sliced mushrooms to the stock. This can be thickened with 1 tablespoon cornflour creamed with a little water, and added 1 hour before serving, but turn the cooker to HIGH after adding it.

2 Soften some onions in oil before starting and put them in the bottom of the cooker, cover with the stock, then proceed as above. Other vegetables such as finely chopped celery, sweet peppers, tomatoes, etc., can also be added, but should be covered by the stock.

Beef and Green Ginger Casserole

This is an idea 'borrowed from' the Chinese who use green ginger very successfully. It is the fresh root which has a good flavour and can be bought in cans at delicatessen shops, and also fresh at Chinese food shops. To keep it in good condition when fresh, peel it, cut into convenient pieces, bottle and cover it with sherry. It will keep for years this way, and the sherry acquires a beautifully spicy flavour, a little of which can be added to almost any meat or poultry casserole, for it gives an added piquancy.

Ingredients (*serves 4*)
1 kg (2¼ lb) lean stewing beef
2 tablespoons oil
2 bayleaves
1 large onion, finely sliced
1 tablespoon flour
pinch of powdered marjoram
600 ml (1 pint) beef stock (cubes will do)
3 pieces of green ginger, walnut size, finely sliced
salt and pepper

Turn the cooker to HIGH for 20 minutes. Trim the beef of fat and gristle, and cut into serving pieces. Heat the oil and add the bayleaves and beef, and brown quickly. Push to one side, then soften the onion. Sprinkle over the flour, and add the marjoram and stock. Let it bubble up before adding the ginger. Season to taste and transfer to the cooker. Cover and cook on LOW for 8–10 hours, or on HIGH for 4–5 hours.

Variation Use chicken instead of beef, but use chicken stock instead of beef and thicken slightly with cornflour (1 tablespoon) creamed in a little water half an hour before serving. Some sliced scallions or spring onions can also be added then, or a can of drained bean sprouts.

Il Garafolato
Roman Beef Stew with cloves and wine. *Garofano* is the Italian for clove.

Ingredients (serves 4–6)
1 kg (2½ lb) lean stewing beef
2 tablespoons olive oil (for authentic flavour)
1 medium onion, sliced
2 cloves garlic, chopped
1 cm (½ in) cinnamon stick
a pinch of nutmeg
6 whole cloves
2 teaspoons chopped parsley
300 ml (½ pint) red wine
3 large peeled tomatoes or equivalent canned
1 cup stock or water
salt and freshly ground pepper

Turn the cooker to HIGH for 20 minutes. Trim and cut the meat into quite large cubes. Heat the oil and brown the meat quickly in it. Add the onion and garlic and cook until they soften but do not colour. Add the cinnamon, nutmeg, cloves and parsley, the wine, and the coarsely chopped tomatoes. Season to taste then add just enough stock or water to barely cover the meat. Cover and cook on LOW for 8–10 hours, or HIGH for 4–5 hours. Thicken with a little flour (1 tablespoon) mixed with water, if you like, but do not make it too thick and lose the flavour.

Hungarian Beef or Goulash
Lamb or pork can also be used.

Ingredients (serves 4–6)
1 kg (2¼ lb) rib beef, boned
seasoned flour
2–3 tablespoons oil
1 large onion, finely sliced
1–2 green or red sweet peppers, or canned, sliced
4 small carrots, thinly sliced
1 tablespoon paprika
½ level teaspoon ground allspice
1 level teaspoon mixed herbs
¼ teaspoon caraway seeds
1 tablespoon tomato purée
300 ml (½ pint) mixed red wine and stock, or all beef stock
salt and freshly ground pepper

To garnish
1 tablespoon plain yoghurt mixed with 1 teaspoon cornflour, or sour cream
chopped parsley

Turn the cooker to HIGH for 20 minutes. Trim the beef, cut into cubes and roll in seasoned flour. Heat the oil and fry quickly all over, then add the onion, carrots, peppers, herbs, paprika, spices, and tomato purée. Add stock and wine and season to taste. Cover and cook for half an hour on HIGH, then on LOW for 6–8 hours, or on HIGH for 4 hours.

Ten minutes before serving, add the yoghurt mixed with the cornflour, or use sour cream if preferred and garnish with parsley.

See also *Beef Goulash Soup*, page 14.

Hawaiian Beef

Lamb or pork can be used instead of beef. This makes a good party dish and can be made some time ahead and reheated.

Ingredients (serves 6–8)

1 kg (2¼ lb) lean stewing beef
1 tablespoon margarine and 1 of oil
2 medium, coarsely chopped onions
1 celery heart, finely chopped
600 ml (1 pint) beef stock (a cube will do)
1 rounded tablespoon tomato chutney, home-made is best

2 level tablespoons cornflour
2 tablespoons soy sauce
1 can pineapple chunks (425 g or 15 oz) size
2 tablespoons wine vinegar
salt and pepper

Turn the cooker to HIGH for 20 minutes. Trim and cube the meat. Heat up the margarine and oil, just soften the onions and celery and put them in the cooker. Add the meat to the oil and brown quickly on all sides before putting it into the cooker. Drain the juice from the pineapple and make it up to 300 ml (½ pint) with water. Season the meat well, then pour in this mixture with the stock. Cover and cook on HIGH for 30 minutes, then on LOW for 6–8 hours, or on HIGH for 4 hours. One hour before it is ready, turn the cooker to HIGH. Mix the cornflour with the vinegar and soy sauce until it is smooth, and when blended add the chutney and mix well. Stir this into the beef and finally add the pineapple chunks. Taste for seasoning. Continue cooking on HIGH. Serve with boiled rice or puréed potatoes.

Japanese Beef

This dish is also known as Teriyaki. It is good served with boiled rice and very crisp, undercooked, shredded cabbage. In Japan it is done with fillet steak.

Ingredients (serves 4–6)

1 kg (2¼ lb) lean chuck steak, cut into very thin slices
1 rounded teaspoon ground ginger
1 tablespoon soft, light brown sugar
2–3 tablespoons oil
150 ml (¼ pint) soy sauce
2 garlic cloves, crushed
225 g (½ lb) mushrooms, sliced
a little butter

Turn the cooker to HIGH for 20 minutes. Put the slices of thin steak between slightly dampened plastic or greaseproof paper, then flatten with a meat bat or wooden rolling pin. Combine all ingredients except the mushrooms and the butter in a bowl and pour over the steak, rubbing it in well. Peel and slice the mushrooms thinly and put into the bottom of the cooker which has been rubbed lightly with butter. Put the steak and marinade on top, cover and cook on LOW for 6–8 hours, or on HIGH for 3–4 hours.

Beef and Kidney Stew or Pie

Ingredients (serves 4–6)

900 g (2 lb) stewing steak
seasoned flour
225 g (½ lb) ox kidney
2–3 tablespoons oil
1 medium onion, sliced
bouquet garni of herbs
1 bayleaf
1 onion Oxo cube
300 ml (½ pint) beef stock
salt and freshly ground pepper

Turn the cooker to HIGH for 20 minutes. Trim the beef, cube and roll it in seasoned flour. Then de-fat and slice the kidney and roll that in the flour as well. Heat the oil and fry both meats quickly on all sides. Push aside and add the onion to just soften it. Add the herbs, crumble up the Oxo cube, and pour in the stock. Let it bubble up, season and transfer to the cooker. Cover and cook on LOW for 6–8 hours, or on HIGH for 3–4. Taste for seasoning. Serve with pastry to make a pie (see below).

Note If using the removable stoneware model, then increase cooking time to 8–10 hours on LOW and 4–5 on HIGH.
Or if this dish is being made for 2 people with half the ingredients, and if using the deep crock-pot, the ingredients can be put into a smaller pot or stoneware jar which fits into the cooker, covered with foil, the lid on top, and cooked with boiling water to half-way up. The cooking times can be reduced to 4–6 on LOW and 2–3 on HIGH.

Pastry 175–225 g (6–8 oz) shortcrust should be rolled out to fit the removable stoneware pot. The pot should be removed with the meat and allowed to cool slightly. Then moisten the edges and put the pastry over, pressing lightly at the edges. Make a slit in the middle to let the steam out, then brush with milk or egg and bake in a hot oven (200°C, 400°F, gas 6) towards the top for about 30 minutes, or until the top is golden.

If your model does not have a removable pot, then put into a pie dish and proceed as above.

Potato topping can also be done the same way, and for a change a mixture of separately cooked turnip (white) or swede and potato, finely puréed together with a scattering of grated cheese on top, is very good.

Mexican Beef (see *Chilli con Carne*, page 77)

Beef Olives

Ingredients (serves 3–4)

6–8 slices raw stewing beef, lean and cut thinly
50 g (2 oz) fresh breadcrumbs
1 small onion, grated
rind of 1 lemon, grated
1 tablespoon mixed chopped parsley and thyme

1 egg
salt and freshly ground pepper
1–2 tablespoons oil
2 tablespoons flour
2 teaspoons tomato purée, optional
300 ml (½ pint) beef stock
4 tablespoons red wine

Turn the cooker to HIGH for 20 minutes. Lay the meat slices between slightly dampened plastic or greaseproof paper and beat them until thin. Mix together the breadcrumbs, onion, lemon rind, herbs, egg and seasoning. Put a little on each beef slice, roll it up and secure either with a skewer or cotton twine. Heat up the oil, quickly brown the parcels on all sides, then shake the flour over and turn them. Add the tomato purée, stock and wine. When it bubbles up, transfer to the cooker and cook on LOW for 6–8 hours or on HIGH for 4–5 hours.

Variation Use thin slices of pork, veal or rashers of gammon bacon. Stuffing mix can also be used if preferred.

Polynesian Beef

Ingredients (serves 6–8)

2 onions, finely sliced
1–1.35 kg (2¼–3 lb) lean, boned, rolled beef or topside, rump, etc.

300 ml (½ pint) pineapple juice, canned
3 tablespoons soy sauce
2 tablespoons oil

1 teaspoon ground ginger
freshly ground pepper and salt
3 carrots, sliced thinly

1 celery heart, sliced thinly
1 tablespoon cornflour

Turn the cooker to HIGH for 20 minutes. Marinate the meat the evening before with the sliced onions, pineapple juice mixed with the soy sauce, ginger, pepper and salt. Heat up the oil and quickly fry the meat, which has been taken out and patted dry, on all sides. Then add the drained and dried onions. First put the onions into the cooker, the carrots and celery heart next, the meat on top, and finally the marinade. Cover, and cook on HIGH for 30 minutes, then on LOW for 10–12 hours, or on HIGH for 5–6 hours. Half an hour before serving, turn to HIGH, and add the cornflour creamed with a little water, stir in, then continue cooking on HIGH until thickened. Serve the meat in thin slices with the sauce.

It is also very good cold, but take any fat from the surface before serving.

Pot Roast

Ingredients (serves 6–8)
1–1.35 kg (2¼–3 lb) top side, rump or brisket
salt and freshly ground pepper
1–2 tablespoons oil
1 large onion, finely sliced

2 medium carrots, finely sliced
2 stalks celery, chopped (optional)
600 ml (1 pint) beef stock
1 tablespoon flour or cornflour
1 bayleaf

Turn the cooker to HIGH for 20 minutes. Trim and if needed tie the joint so that it keeps its shape, season well. Heat up the oil and brown meat all over. Take out, and in the same oil put the bayleaf, onion, carrots and celery and fry until the onion is soft but not coloured. Put the stock in and let it boil, then put this into the cooker and the meat on top. Cover, and cook on LOW for 8–10 hours. When cooked, remove the meat and keep warm, then strain the stock and thicken slightly with 1 tablespoon flour or cornflour creamed with a little cold water. Mix it in well and then bring to the boil stirring all the time.

Serve with freshly cooked carrots, onions or turnips.

See also *Sauerbraten,* page 75.

Potted Beef

This is a very old English method of cooking beef which makes it like a fine beef paste.

Ingredients (serves 6–8)
1 kg (2¼ lb) lean chuck or flank beef
2 tablespoons water
a pinch each of ground mace, and cayenne pepper
salt and freshly ground black pepper
100 g (4 oz) melted butter

Turn the cooker to HIGH for 20 minutes. Trim the meat of all fat or gristle, skin and so on, then rub all over with the spices and seasonings. Put into the cooker with the water, cover and cook on LOW for 10–12 hours or until the beef is really soft and tender. Take it out and chop up finely. Liquidize with the gravy, or put into a food processor such as the Magimix. Process until it is a smooth paste adding a little melted butter if needed. Put it into small pots, and when quite cold pour the rest of the melted butter (a little more may be needed) over the tops, completely covering the meat. If kept in a cold place this potted beef will keep for a few weeks providing the butter seal is not broken.

Beef and Pepper Casserole

This is also good made with chicken: then it is a Roman dish called *Pollo alla Romana con Peperoni*.

Ingredients (serves 4–5)
1 kg (2¼ lb) lean stewing beef
seasoned flour
450 g (1 lb) mixed red, green and if possible yellow sweet peppers
2 tablespoons oil, approximately, olive if possible
450 g (1 lb) peeled tomatoes
1 chopped garlic clove
a pinch chopped rosemary
600 ml (1 pint) beef stock
salt and freshly ground pepper

Turn the cooker to HIGH for 20 minutes. Trim the beef, cut into cubes and roll in seasoned flour. Heat up a tablespoon oil, and put the peppers which have been de-seeded and cut into quarters in it, skin side downwards, and cook over a high flame until the skin blisters all over. Take them out, cool slightly and peel off the skin, then cut into strips. Heat up the remaining oil and quickly fry the beef until it is brown all over, then add the garlic, rosemary, tomatoes, peppers and stock. Season well, bring to the boil and transfer to the cooker. Cover and cook for 8–10 hours on LOW or 4–5 hours on HIGH.

Note The cooking time for chicken is 6–8 hours on LOW and 3–4 hours on HIGH, but if using frozen chicken make sure it is quite thawed out.

Braised Beef with Stuffed Prunes

Ingredients (serves 4–6)
1 kg (2¼ lb) stewing steak
1 large onion, sliced
300 ml (½ pint) dark, draught beer
   or half Guinness and half water
2 tablespoons oil
1 clove garlic, chopped
1 tablespoon flour
225 g (½ lb) prunes, soaked and
   stoned
hazelnuts or almonds,
   approximately 125 g (4 oz)
salt and freshly ground pepper

Turn the cooker to HIGH for 20 minutes. Do not cube the beef, but cut into convenient serving pieces. Heat up the oil and quickly fry the meat all over, and just soften the onion. Add the flour, cook for 1 minute before pouring over the beer, and add the garlic and seasonings. If the sauce seems too thick add a little water and stir well. Transfer to the cooker and cook on LOW for 8–10 hours, or on HIGH for 4–5 hours.

Two hours before it is ready add the prunes, which have had the stones taken out and replaced by a hazelnut, and continue cooking.

Sauerbraten
This is the famous German method of pot-roasting beef.

Ingredients (serves 4–5)
1 kg (2¼ lb) topside or rump beef
salt
1 large onion, sliced
300 ml (½ pint) water
300 ml (½ pint) wine vinegar
1 lemon, unpeeled and sliced
6 whole cloves
3 bayleaves
6 whole black peppercorns
2 tablespoons brown sugar
150 ml (¼ pint) sour cream

Bring the vinegar, water, onion, lemon, sugar, cloves, peppercorns, salt and bayleaves to the boil, then leave to cool. Put the meat into a deep dish and pour the marinade over, cover and leave for 2–3 days, turning every day. Turn the cooker to HIGH for 20 minutes. Then put the meat into the cooker with the strained marinade, cover and cook on LOW for 8–10 hours. Half an hour before it is ready, turn to HIGH and add the sour cream, stirring well. Cover and continue cooking.

Sicilian Beef

To get the full flavour of this dish it is essential that all the vegetables are used.

Ingredients (serves 4–5)

1 kg (2¼ lb) lean stewing beef
seasoned flour
2–3 tablespoons oil
1 fennel bulb, finely sliced
2 green peppers, cored and sliced
1 medium aubergine, cut into
  slices
225 g (½ lb) mushrooms, sliced
salt and pepper

2 tablespoons chopped celery
  leaves
1 large sliced onion
2 garlic cloves, crushed
½ teaspoon ground marjoram
½ teaspoon *herbes de Provence* or
  Italian seasoning
300 ml (½ pint) tomato juice
300 ml (½ pint) beef stock

Turn the cooker to HIGH for 20 minutes. Roll the cubed and trimmed beef in the seasoned flour. Heat the oil and quickly fry it. Prepare all the vegetables and salt the aubergine for 20 minutes in a colander, then wash it and pat dry. Combine all ingredients in the cooker, cover and cook on LOW for 7–8 hours, or HIGH for 3½–4 hours. Taste for seasoning before serving.

Stracotto

This Italian dish is perfect for the slow cooker: the name in English means 'cooked, cooked and more cooked'. In Parma it is used to make a delicious filling for ravioli.

Ingredients (serves 4–6)

1 kg (2¼ lb) lean stewing beef
2 tablespoons oil
1 large onion, sliced
2 celery stalks and leaves, sliced
salt and pepper

1 medium carrot, sliced
1 tablespoon tomato purée
2 whole cloves
4 tablespoons white or red wine
300 ml (½ pint) beef stock

Turn the cooker to HIGH for 20 minutes. Trim the meat of all fat but do not cut it up, except to fit the size of your cooker. Heat the oil, turn the meat quickly and add the vegetables and just soften the onion. Add the tomato purée and the wine and let it bubble up. Pour in the stock, add the cloves and season to taste. Cover and cook on LOW for 8–10 hours, or HIGH for 4–5 hours. If using for a filling such as ravioli or green peppers, chop the mixture finely before using. It also makes a good sauce for pasta.

Swiss Steak

Ingredients (serves 4–5)

1 kg (2¼ lb) stewing beef, either round or rib
seasoned flour
2 tablespoons oil
450 g (1 lb) peeled tomatoes
1 large onion, sliced
2 stalks celery with leaves, chopped
1 tablespoon tomato or apple chutney, preferably home-made
salt and pepper

Turn the cooker to HIGH for 20 minutes. Trim the beef and cut into convenient serving pieces and roll in seasoned flour. Heat the oil and brown the meat quickly all over. Put the onion and celery in the bottom and season. Place the beef on top. Mix the chutney with the tomatoes and pour over the beef. If using fresh tomatoes, add about 150 ml (¼ pint) beef stock. Cover and cook on LOW for 8–10 hours or HIGH for 4–5 hours.

Beef with Walnuts and Orange

Ingredients (serves 4–6)

1 kg (2¼ lb) stewing steak
2 tablespoons oil
8 button onions, if possible, or 2 medium onions, sliced
1 tablespoon flour
salt and pepper
600 ml (1 pint) beef stock
1 celery heart, chopped
1 tablespoon finely shredded orange peel, dried if possible*
150 ml (¼ pint) red wine
a sprig each of thyme, parsley
1 bayleaf
2 cloves garlic, chopped
12 shelled walnuts

Turn the cooker to HIGH for 20 minutes. Cut the meat into large squares and remove any fat or gristle. Heat the oil and quickly fry the meat all over, then the onions until soft, but leave them whole if the button variety. Sprinkle over the flour and add the wine, garlic, and herbs. Season to taste and transfer to the cooker. Cover and cook on LOW for 8–10 hours, but 1 hour before it is ready add the walnuts, finely chopped celery and the grated orange peel if fresh, but finely chopped if dried.

MINCED MEAT DISHES

Chilli con Carne

This is a good Mexican dish which is piquant and spicy. If you don't like food which is hot to the taste, then use only half the chilli powder.

* Keep your orange peels and dry them slowly over the cooker until quite dry. Keep in an airtight jar and use as required.

Ingredients (serves 4–6)
450 g (1 lb) lean minced or
  chopped beef
1 small onion, chopped
1 clove garlic, chopped
1 teaspoon salt
2 teaspoons chilli powder
2 rounded tablespoons tomato
  purée

1 teaspoon ground marjoram or
  oregano
1 can tomatoes, 200 g (7 oz) size,
  chopped
2 cans, 425 g (15 oz) size, drained
  red kidney beans
4 tablespoons tomato juice

Note These quantities are for the 3–3.5 litre (5–6 pint), so if a
smaller cooker is used, only one can of kidney beans will be needed.
Turn the cooker to HIGH for 20 minutes. Heat up a heavy frying
pan and when hot put the beef in, break it up with a fork and
brown all over quickly; pour off any excess fat. Put all ingredients
into the cooker, mixing well, cover and cook on LOW for 6–8 hours
or on HIGH for 3–4 hours.

Serve with rings of raw onion and sliced canned pimentos on a
side dish.

Golubtsy

Russian stuffed cabbage leaves. These can also be made with
minced lamb or cooked bacon or ham.

Ingredients (serves 4)
450 g (1 lb) lean minced meat
12 large cabbage leaves
50 g (2 oz) cooked rice
1 small onion, finely chopped
salt and pepper

1 tablespoon chopped parsley
pinch of mixed herbs or Italian
  seasoning
1 tablespoon brown sugar
1 can tomatoes, 425 g (15 oz) size
½ teaspoon basil

Turn the cooker to HIGH for 20 minutes. Heat up a heavy frying
pan, then put the raw meat in (not if it is already cooked), break it
up with a fork and brown it quickly. Take it out and mix it with the
rice, onion, herbs and seasoning. See that the cabbage leaves are
unmarked, remove the hard stalk. Blanch them in boiling water
for 1–2 minutes, and drain them well on kitchen paper. Divide the
stuffing between them, roll up each leaf like a parcel, tucking in
the ends, and place side by side in the cooker. Chop the tomatoes
coarsely and mix with the brown sugar and the basil; pour over the
rolls. Cover and cook on LOW for 6–8 hours or on HIGH for 3–4
hours.

Meat Ball Casserole

Ingredients (*serves 3–4*)
450 g (1 lb) lean mince
½ cup fresh breadcrumbs
1 small minced onion
1 large beaten egg
a pinch of mace or nutmeg
1 teaspoon mixed herbs or
2 teaspoons fresh chopped parsley
pinch of ground marjoram
a little flour or fine semolina for
  rolling them
salt and pepper

This is the basic meat-ball mixture: all ingredients are mixed well together except the flour or semolina. Shape into small balls about 5 cm (2 in) in diameter with floured hands, then roll the balls in either flour or semolina. See below for variations.

Turn the cooker to HIGH for 20 minutes. Put the meat balls into the cooker, cover and cook on LOW for 4–6 hours. Then add a medium-sized can of condensed vegetable soup made up with a can of water and heated. Cook on HIGH for half an hour.

Or if preferred use tomato purée diluted with water, tomato juice, consommé or good stock, or canned tomatoes.

Variations
1 Add a level tablespoon curry powder to the mixture, also a pinch of fennel seed or crushed cardamom seed, and add 1 teaspoon garam masala (obtainable from Oriental grocers) or curry powder to the soup.

2 1 level tablespoon paprika and ½ teaspoon caraway seeds is another variation.

3 Cook the meat balls in the *Curry Sauce* as given on page 38.

Meat Loaf

Ingredients (*serves 4*)
2 medium beaten eggs
2 slices crustless bread soaked in
  4 tablespoons milk
pinch of ground marjoram and
  mixed herbs
salt and black pepper
1 small onion, grated
675 g (1½ lb) lean minced beef

Turn the cooker to HIGH for 20 minutes. Combine all ingredients in the order given and mix very thoroughly. Either shape into a round or put into a greased tin which fits your cooker, and stand on a trivet or jam jar lid, covered with foil. If the latter, pour boiling water around up to half-way up. Cook on LOW for 6–8 hours or on HIGH for 3–4 hours. Serve either hot or cold; if hot the following sauce can be made and poured over the meat, the cooker turned to HIGH and cooked for 15–20 minutes.

Barbecue Sauce (1) Mix together 2 tablespoons brown sugar, ½ teaspoon paprika powder, 1 tablespoon tomato purée, 2 tablespoons red wine vinegar, 1 teaspoon dry mustard powder, a few drops of Worcestershire sauce and 2 tablespoons tomato chutney (home-made is best). Pour this over the meat loaf and cook at HIGH for 15–20 minutes.

Turkish Meat Loaf
Lamb is also used.

Ingredients (*serves 6*)
1 kg (2¼ lb) minced beef
2 medium grated onions
1 level teaspoon each of ground coriander, cinnamon, cumin and allspice
2 tablespoons tomato purée
2 beaten eggs
4 tablespoons finely chopped parsley

salt and freshly ground black pepper
3 tablespoons red wine or stock
a little butter or margarine

To garnish
150 g (5 oz) plain yoghurt

Turn the cooker to HIGH for 20 minutes. Mix all ingredients except the butter together very well, then lightly grease the cooker with butter or margarine, or use a tin which fits the cooker and grease that. Put the mixture either into the cooker or a tin. Cover with foil, and if using a tin it should be stood on a small trivet or jam jar lid and boiling water poured around to half-way up. Cover and cook on LOW for 6–8 hours, or HIGH for 3–4 hours.

Serve either hot or cold with cold, plain yoghurt over the top.

Moussaka
This is a good Greek dish which should be made with minced lamb but beef can be used. If aubergines are hard to get, then blanched cauliflower sprigs can be used.

Ingredients (*serves 4–5*)
2 medium aubergines
salt

4 tablespoons oil
1 medium onion, chopped
1 200 g (7 oz) can tomatoes

a pinch of nutmeg
675 g (1½ lb) minced meat
2 beaten eggs
150 ml (¼ pint) creamy milk
2 tablespoons hard cheese, grated

Turn the cooker to HIGH for 20 minutes. Slice the aubergines, sprinkle with salt and leave in a colander for about 20 minutes; then wash them under the cold water tap and pat dry. Heat the oil and fry them until soft, but do not brown them. Arrange half the aubergine at the bottom of the cooker. Fry the onion and the meat until lightly browned, season and drain off excess fat. Put a layer of meat on top of the aubergine. Drain the tomatoes, and coarsely chop. Sprinkle half the nutmeg over the meat, then put a layer of tomatoes on top. Repeat this until all ingredients are used. Beat together the eggs, milk and cheese and pour this over, evenly. Cover and cook on LOW for 4–6 hours or HIGH for 2–3 hours.

Stuffed Peppers, Marrow or Courgettes

Use the stuffing given on page 78 for *Golubtsy*, having first removed the seeds and in the case of the marrow and courgettes, cut in half lengthways. (If using a shallow crock-pot then cut peppers in half lengthways too.) Put the stuffed vegetables in the cooker which has been preheated on HIGH for 20 minutes, and add either a medium can of consommé or 1 tablespoon tomato purée diluted with 300 ml (½ pint) water. Top the vegetables with a sprinkling of grated hard cheese. Cook on LOW for 6–8 hours or HIGH for 3–4 hours.

See also *Sauces* in Index.

LAMB OR MUTTON

As a name 'mutton' has gone out of fashion nowadays, but in fact we often eat it for it is the meat of a sheep over one year old. Up until three-years-old sheep meat can be roasted with success and in fact has more flavour than the younger meat. The slow cooker is perfect for this meat and there are many ways of cooking it.

See *Roasting of Meats*, page 62.

China Cholla

This dish dates from the time of the East India Company, and is a pleasant dish to serve on a summer's evening.

Ingredients (serves 4–6)
1 kg (2¼ lb) neck of lamb or
  shoulder
2 small lettuces
4 spring onions or scallions
450 g (1 lb) shelled peas
salt and freshly ground pepper
a sprig each of thyme and mint
  chopped
½ teaspoon ground coriander

1 teaspoon sugar
1 tablespoon butter
300 ml (½ pint) stock
175 g (6 oz) button mushrooms
1 small cucumber

To garnish
1 small onion, finely sliced
1 tablespoon chopped parsley

Turn the cooker to HIGH for 20 minutes. Trim the meat of fat and bone and cut into small pieces. Shred the lettuce, and chop the spring onions. Put all ingredients into the cooker, except the mushrooms and cucumber. Season well, cover and cook on LOW for 6–8 hours, or HIGH for 3–4 hours. One hour before it is ready, turn cooker to HIGH and add the cucumber, peeled and sliced, and the button mushrooms, pushing them down into the liquid, then continue cooking. Serve with thin slices of raw onion and chopped parsley on top with boiled rice.

Irish Stew

This is very similar to Lancashire hot-pot, and both should be thick and creamy, not swimming in liquid.

Ingredients (serves about 4)
1 kg (2¼ lb) middle neck of lamb
  chops or shoulder chops
2 large onions, finely sliced
2 bayleaves
1 kg (2¼ lb) potatoes, finely sliced
salt and pepper

1 tablespoon chopped parsley
  and thyme, mixed
300 ml (½ pint) boiling water or
  white stock

To garnish
1 tablespoon chopped parsley

Turn the cooker to HIGH for 20 minutes. Trim the meat of fat, skin and bone and cut into fairly large pieces. Put the bones on to boil, covered with water and with salt and pepper. Put layers of the potato, onion and meat in the cooker, seasoning each layer as you go and also sprinkling over some of the herbs. Finish with a layer of potato. Strain the bone stock and pour over 300 ml (½ pint) of it. Cover and cook on LOW for 8–10 hours or on HIGH for 4–5 hours. Garnish with the chopped parsley.

Variation If rashers of gammon bacon and sausages are used instead of the lamb, then this dish becomes *Dublin Coddle,* and chicken stock should be used.

Lamb with Apples and Cider

Ingredients (*serves 6–8*)
1.5 kg (3¼ lb) boned loin or lean shoulder lamb
juice and peel of 1 lemon
450 g (1 lb) cooking apples
2 tablespoons brown sugar
2 cloves garlic
1 tablespoon ground ginger
1 teaspoon ground cloves
salt and pepper
600 ml (1 pint) cider or apple juice

Turn the cooker to HIGH for 20 minutes. See that the meat is not too fatty. Then rub the lamb on all sides with the lemon juice and sprinkle the inside with the peel. Cover with the peeled and cored apples and sprinkle with sugar. Season well before rolling up and securing with skewers or cotton twine. Sliver the garlic and insert under the skin.

Mix together the ginger, cloves, salt and pepper and rub this all over the skin of the lamb. Stand on a small trivet in the cooker and pour the boiling cider or apple juice around. Cover and cook on LOW for 8–10 hours, or HIGH for 4–5 hours. Take any excess fat from the juices, and thicken if you like with a little flour creamed in water; it is extremely good unthickened.

Lamb Curry
See *Duck Korma*, page 47.

Lamb and Kidney Wine Casserole

Ingredients (*serves 4*)
4 lean lamb chops
4 lamb's kidneys
2–3 tablespoons oil
1 medium onion, sliced
1 medium carrot, sliced
pinch of chopped rosemary
½ teaspoon tarragon
generous 300 ml (½ pint) half red wine and half water
1 leek, sliced
salt and freshly ground pepper

Turn the cooker to HIGH for 20 minutes. Trim the chops of excess fat. Skin the kidneys, cut in half and remove the fatty cores. Heat up oil and quickly fry both meats on all sides. Peel and slice the onion, leek and carrot and put them at the bottom of the cooker, seasoned, and with half the herbs. Then put the lamb and kidney on top, season and scatter over the remaining herbs and add the wine and water. Cover and cook on HIGH for 6 hours, or on LOW for 10–12 hours.

Lamb with Lentils

Ingredients (serves 4)

1 kg (2¼ lb) lean lamb
225 g (½ lb) brown lentils soaked
   overnight
2 celery stalks, finely sliced
2 garlic cloves, sliced
2 carrots, finely sliced
1 large onion, sliced

3 ripe tomatoes, peeled and sliced
1 level teaspoon Italian seasoning
   or mixed herbs
½ teaspoon ground coriander
600 ml (1 pint) approximately,
   boiling water
salt and pepper

Soak the brown lentils overnight and drain.

Turn the cooker to HIGH for 20 minutes. Trim the meat and remove any excess fat and bone, then cube it. Put all ingredients into the cooker and see that the liquid is about 2.5 cm (1 in) above the lentils. Season well, cover and cook on LOW for 10–12 hours, or HIGH for 5–6 hours.

Variations

1 This can also be done with leftover boiled ham or bacon with sausages (smoked) added.

2 Pieces or joints of game are excellent done this way.

Lamb with Spinach and Yoghurt

This is a good Greek dish called *Kreas me Spanaki.*

Ingredients (serves 6–8)

1 kg (2¼ lb) lean lamb
2 tablespoons oil
1 tablespoon tomato purée,
   dissolved in 300 ml (½ pint)
   boiling water
3 medium onions, chopped

½ teaspoon powdered marjoram
1 kg (2¼ lb) washed spinach, or
   equivalent frozen
salt and pepper

To garnish
300 ml (½ pint) plain yoghurt

Turn the cooker to HIGH for 20 minutes. Trim the lamb of fat and bone and cut up into cubes; heat the oil and quickly fry it. Then soften the onions and put them in the bottom of the cooker with the meat on top. Dissolve the tomato purée in the water. Sprinkle the marjoram over the meat and pour the tomato over all. Cover and cook at LOW for 8–10 hours or HIGH for 4–5 hours. One hour before it is ready add the spinach, pressing it down well. Cover and continue cooking at HIGH.

Season before serving and spoon the yoghurt over, allowing it to just heat through and set for about 5–10 minutes.

Norman Lamb Casserole

Ingredients (serves 4–6)
4–6 shoulder chops
1 tablespoon oil
2 medium onions, sliced
1 large red pepper, sliced
4 fennel stalks or ½ teaspoon, dried
½ teaspoon chopped rosemary
1 tablespoon chopped parsley
pinch of lovage
1 onion Oxo cube dissolved in
    300 ml (½ pint) water
300 ml (½ pint) dry cider
225 g (½ lb) sliced mushrooms

Turn the cooker to HIGH for 20 minutes. Trim the chops so that they are not fatty, and season all over. Prepare the vegetables and put them in the cooker with the herbs and the dissolved stock cube. Heat the oil and brown the chops. Add the cider, let it boil and then transfer to the cooker. Cook on LOW for 8 hours, or HIGH for 4 hours, then taste for seasoning and add the sliced mushrooms. Thicken with 1 tablespoon of flour if you like, cover and cook again for 1–2 hours on LOW or 1 hour on HIGH.

Variations

1 Add 1 can of butter or baked beans, or 225 g (½ lb) whole green beans, and cook for a further ½ hour at HIGH.

2 Add 4 or 6 sliced kidneys with the chops, browning them first. In both these variations it will stretch the meal to 6–8 people.

Leg of Mutton à l'étuvée
This is a good way to cook mutton.

Ingredients (serves 6–8)
1 small leg mutton
2 tablespoons oil
150 ml (¼ pint) red wine
1 medium-size can consommé
1 medium onion, sliced
1 bayleaf
sprig of thyme
salt and freshly ground pepper

For the sauce
1 glass red wine
150 ml (¼ pint) cream

Turn the cooker to HIGH for 20 minutes. Heat the oil and brown the meat all over in it. Soften the onion and put it in the bottom of the cooker. Put the meat back into the frying pan, season and pour over the red wine and the consommé, adding the bayleaf and thyme. Transfer to the cooker, cover and cook at LOW for 10–12 hours, or HIGH for 5–6 hours. When cooked, put the meat on to a warmed dish and keep warm. Strain the sauce and reduce it on top of the stove with the red wine to about half. Taste for seasoning, then add the cream slowly, stirring all the time. Heat it up but do not reboil.

Persian Lamb

Ingredients (serves 6)

1 kg (2¼ lb) lean lamb
2 tablespoons oil
1 medium onion, sliced
175 g (6 oz) soaked dried apricots
1 tablespoon raisins or sultanas
225 g (½ lb) half-cooked long grain rice
1 level teaspoon ground cinnamon

½ teaspoon ground coriander
water (approximately 900 ml or 1½ pints)
1 lemon, thinly sliced

To garnish

1 tablespoon sliced almonds and chopped parsley

Turn the cooker to HIGH for 20 minutes. Trim the meat and cube it. Heat the oil and soften the onion in it, take out and put in the meat and spices and quickly brown all over. Drain the apricots and add them and the dried fruit. Pour over about 600 ml (1 pint) of the hot water. Lightly oil the cooker, then layer it with the half-cooked rice, and the meat and fruit mixture, finishing with the rice. Pour remaining liquid over and cook on LOW for 8–10 hours or 4–5 on HIGH. Half an hour before it is ready put the thinly sliced unpeeled lemon on top and continue cooking. Serve with the almonds and parsley scattered over.

Variation Use pork instead of lamb.

Pilaff of Lamb

This is a good dish in which to use up leftover meats or poultry of all kinds. If using fresh meats, increase cooking time by two hours.

Ingredients (serves 4)

450 g (1 lb) lean, cooked lamb, chopped
1 medium onion, finely sliced
1 medium sweet pepper, seeded and sliced
½ teaspoon powdered marjoram
pinch of chopped rosemary

100 g (4 oz) button mushrooms, whole
175 g (6 oz) easy-cook long grain rice or half-cooked rice
1 tablespoon pine-nut kernels, (pinoli) optional
1 can tomatoes, 200 g (7 oz) size
600 ml (1 pint) chicken stock

Turn the cooker to HIGH for 20 minutes. Mix all ingredients together, and put into the cooker. Cover and cook on LOW for 6–8 hours or on HIGH for 3–4 hours.

Rosemary Spiced Lamb

Ingredients (serves 6–8)
1.5–1.75 kg (3–3½ lb) leg of lamb
2 cloves garlic, chopped
salt and pepper
1 tablespoon mustard powder
1 teaspoon chopped rosemary
   leaves, fresh if possible
½ teaspoon Schwartz lamb
   seasoning
pinch of ground ginger
1 tablespoon lemon juice
1 medium can consommé, boiling

This recipe is for the 2.5–3.5 litre (4–6 pint) cooker; for the smaller crock-pots either buy a smaller joint or have a 1.5 kg (3 lb) one boned.

Turn the cooker to HIGH for 20 minutes. Trim any excess fat from the meat. Cut the garlic into thin slivers, make holes in the flesh of the meat and insert the garlic into them. Mix all the other ingredients except the consommé together and rub this over the flesh and the skin. Put the meat on a trivet in the cooker and pour the hot consommé around. Cover and cook on LOW for 10–12 hours or HIGH for 5–6 hours. Carve the meat on a warmed dish, take off any excess fat from the gravy and serve separately.

Saffron Lamb Casserole

Saffron is very expensive nowadays but gives an unmistakable and lovely flavour. If not available use 1 level teaspoon turmeric mixed with 2 teaspoons honey.

Ingredients (serves 4)
1 kg (2¼ lb) lean leg lamb chopped
   into 5 cm (2 in) pieces
2 tablespoons oil
6 medium cloves of garlic
½ teaspoon saffron, or see above
1 tablespoon paprika
1 tablespoon flour
300 ml (½ pint) white wine
300 ml (½ pint) white stock
salt and pepper

To garnish
1 tablespoon fresh mint, chopped

Turn the cooker to HIGH for 20 minutes. Pulp the garlic and mix it with the saffron and add the paprika. Heat the oil and quickly brown the meat all over. Shake the flour over the meat, turning the cubes, add the garlic mixture, the wine and stock. Season to taste, cover and cook on LOW for 8–10 hours or HIGH for 4–5 hours. Garnish with the fresh, chopped mint before serving.

Shanks of Lamb, Spiced

This is a pleasant method of cooking the quite inexpensive lamb shanks. The same recipe can also be used for chicken or turkey legs.

Ingredients (serves 4)
4 lamb shanks
1 teaspoon each of ground cumin and ground coriander
1 can tomatoes, 425 g (15 oz) size
150 ml (¼ pint) dry white wine or dry cider
1 teaspoon *herbes de Provence* or Italian seasoning
1 large onion, sliced
salt and freshly ground pepper
1 can creamed mushrooms, 212 g (7½ oz) size

Turn the cooker to HIGH for 20 minutes. Rub the shanks with the mixed cumin and coriander and put into the cooker. Then mix the herbs with the tomatoes and onion and put on top. Season all to taste then add the wine. Cover and cook on LOW for 8–10 hours or on HIGH for 4–5 hours. Half an hour before it is ready, add the can of creamed mushrooms, stir well and finish the cooking on HIGH.

Spanish Lamb Casserole

Ingredients (serves 4)
1 kg (2¼ lb) trimmed neck lamb
2 tablespoons oil
1 large onion, sliced
1 green pepper, seeded and sliced
50 g (2 oz) rice
1 medium can tomatoes
600 ml (1 pint) stock
8 black olives
1 cup cooked peas
salt and pepper
1 egg
1 teaspoon olive oil
a few drops wine vinegar

Turn the cooker to HIGH for 20 minutes. Trim and cube the lamb. Heat the oil and quickly fry the meat; put it into the cooker. Fry the onion in the same oil until soft, then add the pepper and, when soft, the rice. Cook for about 2 minutes and add the tomatoes and the stock. Season to taste, cover and cook on LOW for 8–10 hours or HIGH for 4–5 hours. Half an hour before it is ready, turn to HIGH and add the olives and peas, mixing them in and continue cooking.

Just before serving, beat the egg with the olive oil and vinegar, stir into the hot stew and serve at once.

See also *Boeuf à la Mode*, page 63, *Beef with Beans*, page 65, *Hawaiian Beef*, page 70, *Hungarian Beef*, page 69, *Moussaka*, page 80, *Turkish Meat Loaf*, page 80.

PORK

For roasting instructions see page 63. Thick pork chops can be slit across the centre (not quite through), stuffed with stuffing given below, put on to a rack brushed with oil and cooked on LOW for 6–8 hours.

Braised Pork Chops Savoy

Ingredients (serves 4)
4 thick, lean pork chops
2 teaspoons grated lemon peel
1 tablespoon oil
1 medium onion, sliced
2 large cooking apples, peeled, cored and sliced
1 tablespoon brown sugar
2 tablespoons sultanas
salt and pepper
300 ml (½ pint) dry cider

Turn the cooker to HIGH for 20 minutes. Trim the chops of fat and rub the lemon peel all over them. Heat the oil and quickly brown them on all sides. Put aside and just soften the onion in the oil, and put them both into the cooker. Add all the other ingredients, mixing them well. Cover and cook on LOW for 8–10 hours, or 4–5 on HIGH.

Braised Stuffed Pork Steaks (Fillets)

Ingredients (serves 2–4)
1 large, or 2 small pork steaks, seasoned
a little oil or butter
1 large onion, finely sliced
4 carrots, sliced
pinch mixed herbs
300 ml (½ pint) meat stock

For the stuffing (or use a packet)
2 cups fresh breadcrumbs
1 teaspoon each: chopped sage and thyme
finely grated peel and juice of 1 lemon
a pinch mace
2 tablespoons milk
1 small grated onion
1 tablespoon chopped parsley
salt and pepper
1 tablespoon melted butter or margarine

Mix all the stuffing ingredients together, and if it seems very stiff, then add a little more milk, but do not make it sloppy.

Turn the cooker to HIGH for 20 minutes. First prepare the pork steaks by slitting down the centre with a sharp knife, but do not cut through the meat on the bottom. The two flaps are then opened gradually by pulling gently, so that it opens out to a flat shape. Trim off any pieces of fat and season the inside well.

There are two ways of stuffing the steaks: either put the stuffing on the flat piece and put the other side, or pork steak on top, or stuff and roll up like a Swiss roll. Either way see that it is secured by skewers or cotton twine so that the stuffing doesn't fall out.

Rub the chops with oil or soft butter and season the outside. On the bottom of the cooker lay a bed of onion and carrots, with the herbs. Cover with the stock and put the pork steaks on top. Cover and cook for 8–10 hours on LOW or 4–5 hours on HIGH.

Variations

1 Use either red or white wine or cider instead of the stock, and add the grated peel of 1 orange.

2 Add 1 whole orange, unpeeled but cut into quarters.

Roast, Stuffed Pork Steaks

Follow the instructions given for *Braised Pork Steaks*, but first brown quickly in a little oil, then sprinkle with flour and stand on a trivet in the cooker with just 4 tablespoons of stock, wine, or cider in the bottom. Or they can be cooked with a *Sweet-sour Sauce*, see page 107.

Cassoulet

This is a filling and delicious French bean casserole ideally suited to the slow cooker. Halve ingredients for the 2 litre (3¼ pint).

Ingredients (serves about 8)

450 g (1 lb) dried haricot beans soaked overnight

2 tablespoons tomato purée, optional

3 cloves garlic, chopped

a sprig of thyme, marjoram and parsley, all chopped

1 bayleaf

2 medium onions, chopped

450 g (1 lb) lean pork, cut into cubes

4–6 slices salami

salt and pepper

1 glass red wine

Turn the cooker to HIGH for 20 minutes. Wash the soaked beans and put into the cooker barely covered with cold water and cook either on LOW for 6–8 hours or on HIGH for 2–3 hours, until they are tender. Put into a bowl, draining but reserving the liquid. Brown the meat quickly all over in a frying pan, transfer to the cooker with all the other ingredients. Add the beans, mixing well, and add enough of the liquid to cover. Put the lid on and cook at LOW for a further 8–10 hours.

In France this is finished with a layer of freshly grated breadcrumbs which form a crust and soak up the juices. Scatter the crumbs over about 15 minutes before serving, cover and continue cooking on HIGH.

Variation Wings, legs and so on of duck, turkey, goose or chicken can also be added to the cassoulet. If cooked, then add them at half-time. Some sausages are good too, but if the unsmoked kind they should be lightly grilled or fried first to give them colour.

Mexican Pork Chops

Ingredients (serves 4)
4 pork chops
1 tablespoon oil
1 green pepper, seeded and sliced
1 large onion, sliced
¼ teaspoon chilli powder
4 tablespoons raw rice
pinch of sage and thyme
1 can tomatoes, 425 g (15 oz) size
salt and freshly ground pepper

Turn the cooker to HIGH for 20 minutes. Trim the chops of any excess fat; heat the oil and brown them quickly. Put a mixture of the onion, chilli powder and pepper in the bottom of the cooker, the chops on top and then the rice and herbs, all seasoned. Pour over the tomatoes which have been coarsely chopped and add either 3–4 tablespoons water, stock or tomato juice. Cover and cook on LOW for 8–10 hours or HIGH for 4–5 hours.

Pâté of Pork, French Country Style

Ingredients (makes about 10 slices)
450 g (1 lb) streaky pork, keep the skin
225 g (½ lb) breast veal
225 g (½ lb) beef
2 garlic cloves
pinch of sage
3 tablespoons brandy
2 egg yolks
2 bayleaves
salt and pepper

Get a suitable-sized dish which fits the cooker and a small trivet. The pâté can be cooked directly in the cooker, but it's impossible to get out easily.

Turn the cooker to HIGH for 20 minutes. Remove any bone, gristle or skin from the meat. Take off the pork skin in one piece and line the bottom of the dish with it. Mince the veal, beef and garlic together, but chop the pork into tiny dice. Beat the egg yolks and add them to the veal and beef and season. Pour the brandy over the pork and let it marinate a while, with the sage and 1 bayleaf.

On top of the pork fat put a layer of the minced meats, then a layer of pork, then the minced meats and so on until it is all used, ending with a layer of pork. Put the remaining bayleaf on top, and add any of the brandy marinade which remains. Cover with foil, put into the cooker and pour boiling water up to half-way. Cover and cook for 8–10 hours on LOW or 4–5 on HIGH. Take out and cool quickly, weighting it. Serve cold, cut into thick slices, with crusty bread or dry toast.

Persian Pork
See *Persian Lamb*, page 86.

Pork Chops and Corn Casserole

Ingredients (*serves 4*)
4 pork chops, or 1 large pork steak cut into rounds
salt, pepper and a little dried sage
1 can whole kernel corn 425 g (15 oz) size
1 small onion, chopped

1 green pepper, seeded and chopped and 1 red pepper, seeded and chopped
½ teaspoon chilli powder or cayenne pepper

To garnish
2 tablespoons chopped parsley

Turn the cooker to HIGH for 20 minutes. Trim the chops of fat, or cut the trimmed pork steak into rounds. Rub them with salt, pepper and the sage. Mix all other ingredients together and put into the cooker. Lay the pork on top. Cover and cook on LOW for 6–8 hours, or HIGH for 3–4 hours.

Pork and Pineapple
See *Duck with Pineapple* (*Po Lo Chiang*), page 49, and cut the pork into large chunks before cooking.

Pork Pot Roast with Leeks

Ingredients (*serves 6–8*)
1–1.5 kg (2¼–3 lb) lean roasting pork (leg, loin, etc.)
1 tablespoon oil
1 clove garlic
2 medium onions

4 large leeks
1 bayleaf
2 fresh sage leaves or ½ teaspoon dried
300 ml (½ pint) hot stock or water
salt and pepper

Turn the cooker to HIGH for 20 minutes. Tie the pork into a convenient shape; heat the oil and brown it all over. Slice the onions and garlic, clean the leeks well and cut into chunks including part of the green. Put these at the bottom of the cooker and add the stock or water, and season. Put the bayleaf under the pork and the pork on top of the vegetables. Sprinkle with salt, pepper and the sage. Cover and cook on LOW for 10–12 hours, or HIGH for 5–6 hours.

Pork, Roast with Honey and Cranberries

Ingredients (serves 6–8)
1–1.5 kg (2¼–3 lb) roasting pork
salt and pepper
125 g (4 oz) chopped cranberries
pinch of ground cloves
pinch of ground allspice

4 tablespoons honey
1 teaspoon grated orange peel
4 tablespoons orange juice
pinch of mace
salt and pepper

Turn the cooker to HIGH for 20 minutes. Tie the roast into a convenient shape, rub with salt and pepper and put into the cooker. Combine all the other ingredients and pour over the meat. Cover and cook at LOW for 10–12 hours or HIGH for 5–6 hours. This is also a good way of cooking ham which has been soaked overnight. If cranberries are difficult to get, gooseberries or black cherries can also be used.

Elizabethan Ragout of Pork
This is a seventeenth-century recipe for pork that is perhaps past its prime.

Ingredients (serves 6–8)
1–1.5 kg (2¼–3½ lb) boneless pork,
   not fat
2 tablespoons oil
1 tablespoon flour
1 celery heart, chopped
3 medium onions, chopped

3 medium eating apples, chopped
125 g (¼ lb) seedless white grapes
1 orange, quartered
sprig each of sage and parsley
½ bottle red wine
salt and pepper

Turn the cooker to HIGH for 20 minutes. Heat the oil and brown the meat all over in it. Lightly soften the onions, celery and apples, and put them in the cooker. Rub the pork in salt, pepper and flour and put on top. Then add all the other ingredients, seeing that the orange is without pith or pip. Pour the wine over, and add a little water if it doesn't half cover the meat. Cover and cook on LOW for 10–12 hours, or HIGH for 5–6 hours.

Roast Pork with Orange

Ingredients (serves 6)
1 roasting joint of pork about
   1–1.5 kg (2¼–3½ lb)
1 teaspoon powdered sage
1 cup boiling water
salt and pepper

2 oranges
150 ml (¼ pint) dry sherry or
   white wine
1–2 tablespoons redcurrant or
   apple jelly

Turn the cooker to HIGH for 20 minutes. Rub the pork with salt, pepper and sage. Put it into the cooker and grate the peel of 1 orange over the top. Add the remaining oranges (unpeeled) cut into quarters and all the other ingredients except the jelly. Cook on LOW for 10–12 hours and half an hour before it is ready stir in the jelly, taste for seasoning and continue cooking. Serve with the oranges around the meat, and skim off any excess fat from the gravy before dishing up.

See also *Beef with Beans*, page 65, *Paprika Chicken*, page 41, *Chinese Chicken*, page 35, *Hawaiian Beef*, page 70, *Honeyed Chicken*, page 38, and *Turkey with Cherries*, page 52.

HAM

The slow cooker is very good for boiling ham, bacon and also tongue. It does not shrink and the shape remains the same, making it much easier to carve. According to the shape and size of your cooker decide the most convenient joints for cooking, and either skewer or tie them securely.

Test with a fork at the minimum cooking time to see if the meat is done, but do not worry about an extra hour for it will not spoil.

Boiled Bacon or Ham

Also for tongue.

It is important that bacon, ham or tongue is soaked for at least 8 hours before cooking, and the water poured away.

Ingredients (serves 4–6)

1 joint of bacon or ham, about 1–1.5 kg (2¼–3 lb)
1 teaspoon sugar
1 bayleaf
juice and skin of ½ lemon
a few peppercorns and 2–3 whole cloves for ham
a sprig of parsley
boiling water or cider to cover

Turn the cooker to HIGH for 20 minutes. Put the joint and all the ingredients into the cooker, adding the boiling water or cider last. Cover and cook on HIGH for 1–2 hours, then turn to LOW and cook for 10–12 hours. Or cook on HIGH for 5–6 hours. Allow to cool in the cooker, unless serving it hot. See *Glazed Corned Beef*, page 66.

Ham and Apricot Hot-Pot

This can also be done with leftover cold bacon or ham.

Ingredients (serves 4)

4 thick gammon rashers or ham steaks, soaked for 2 hours
225 g (½ lb) dried, soaked apricots or fresh, stoned apricots
1 rounded tablespoon sultanas

6 medium-size half-cooked
potatoes, peeled and sliced

300 ml (½ pint) stock
salt and pepper

Turn the cooker to HIGH for 20 minutes. Drain the gammon and apricots and lay the gammon in the bottom of the cooker, then put the apricots and sultanas on top. Cover with the stock, adding a little more if needed. Put the peeled and sliced potatoes on top, seasoning to taste. Cover with foil, then the lid and cook at HIGH for half an hour, then on LOW for 6–8 hours, or HIGH for 3–4 hours. If using the removable crock-pot the potatoes can be browned in the oven or under the grill.

Ham or Bacon Loaf

Leftovers can be used, and if there is less than the amount of ham given then either make up with more sausagemeat or adjust other ingredients.

Ingredients (serves about 6)
1 medium grated onion
450 g (1 lb) finely minced or
chopped cooked ham or bacon
225 g (½ lb) sausagemeat
1 cup fresh white breadcrumbs
freshly ground black pepper

1 tablespoon mustard powder
½ teaspoon dried tarragon
1 tablespoon fresh, chopped
parsley
1 large beaten egg
150 ml (¼ pint) hot stock or milk

Turn the cooker to HIGH for 20 minutes. Grease a suitable bowl that will fit easily into the cooker. Mix all ingredients together thoroughly, adding the egg and stock or milk last. Do not make it too sloppy, and let it rest for about half an hour so that the breadcrumbs can absorb the liquid. Put into the bowl, cover with foil, then pour boiling water to half-way up the side. Cover and cook on HIGH for 1 hour, then on LOW for 6–8 hours, or on HIGH for 4 hours. It can be served hot or cold, cut into thick slices.

Irish Ham Roll

Ingredients (serves 4–6)
4–6 slices of ham or bacon, cooked,
and not too thin
1 cup chopped walnuts

1 cup raisins or sultanas soaked
for 2–3 hours in cider
1 can tomatoes, 290 g (7 oz) size
salt and pepper

Turn the cooker to HIGH for 20 minutes. Mix the soaked raisins and nuts together; spread on the ham or bacon slices, roll them up and secure. Put them, seam side down, closely packed in the cooker. Pour the tomatoes, which have been seasoned and coarsely chopped, with the juice over the top. Cook at HIGH for 3–4 hours, or LOW for 6–8 hours.

Scalloped Ham

Ingredients (*serves 6*)
6 slices of ham or lean cooked bacon
6 medium potatoes, peeled and sliced
1 medium onion, chopped
100 g (4 oz) grated hard cheese, like Cheddar
1 medium can asparagus or celery soup
pinch of paprika

Turn the cooker to HIGH for 20 minutes. Prepare the sliced vegetables. Put half the ham, potatoes and onion, and cheese in layers, in the cooker. Repeat this until all is used up, then cover with the undiluted soup, seeing that it is spread evenly over all. Sprinkle the paprika over, cover and cook on LOW for 8 hours or HIGH for 4 hours.

See also *Pork with Honey and Cranberries*, page 93, *Duck with Orange and Irish Mist*, page 48, *Braised Veal Catalane*, below

VEAL

The cheaper cuts of veal, such as flank, breast, neck or shoulder cook perfectly in the slow cooker. You can also make a wonderful *Osso Buco* with shin of veal. Many of the chicken recipes are good for veal.

Braised Veal Catalane

Ingredients (*serves 4–6*)
1 kg (2¼ lb) breast, flank, etc., veal
2–3 tablespoons oil
1 medium onion, sliced
2 cloves garlic, chopped
175 g (6 oz) mushrooms, sliced
1 medium green pepper, seeded and sliced
pinch of tarragon, and parsley
1 can tomatoes, small size
pinch of saffron, optional
1 tablespoon flour
1 glass white wine, about 4 tablespoons
300 ml (½ pint) white stock, hot
salt and pepper

To garnish
12 green or black olives, stoned
1 tablespoon chopped parsley

Turn the cooker to HIGH for 20 minutes. Trim and cut the meat into large cubes; heat up the oil and fry it quickly all over. Push aside and add the onions and soften them. Add all ingredients and season to taste. Cover and cook on HIGH for half an hour, then on LOW for 6–8 hours or on HIGH for 4 hours.

Garnish with the olives and parsley, and turn to HIGH for about 10 minutes to heat them through.

Note This recipe is very good made with pork instead of veal.

Fricandeau of Veal

A fricandeau used to be a special cut, shaped rather like a rectangular cushion, but a boned shoulder of about 1.5 kg (3 lb) in weight does very well.

Ingredients (serves 6–8)
1–1.5 kg (2¼–3 lb) boned shoulder of veal
225 g (½ lb) streaky bacon rashers
2–3 medium carrots
3 cloves garlic, chopped

1 bouquet garni
2 small onions
300 ml (½ pint) white stock, hot
1 tablespoon potato flour or cornflour
salt and pepper

Turn the cooker to HIGH for 20 minutes. Trim the veal and tie into shape, then wrap entirely in the rashers. Slice the vegetables finely and put into the cooker with the bouquet garni. Put the meat on top and pour the stock over. Season to taste, cover and cook on HIGH for 1 hour, then on LOW for 8–10 hours or on HIGH for 4–5 hours. Half an hour before it is ready mix the potato flour or cornflour with a little water and paint the top of the meat with this. Cover and continue cooking.

Galantine of Veal

Ingredients (serves about 8)
1 boned breast of veal in one piece
450 g (1 lb) sausagemeat
1 hard-boiled egg
chopped tarragon, parsley and thyme

grated peel of 1 lemon
salt and pepper
300 ml (½ pint) white stock or mixed stock and white wine, boiling

Turn the cooker to HIGH for 20 minutes. Lay the veal flat; mix the sausagemeat with the herbs, lemon peel, salt and pepper. Slice the egg, then put the sausagemeat stuffing over the veal, adding the sliced egg along the centre. Roll up and secure either with skewers or cotton twine and put into the cooker. Pour the boiling stock or wine over, seeing that it almost covers the galantine. Cover and cook for 1 hour on HIGH, then on LOW for 8–10 hours. When cool take out of the stock, put into a dish which just fits, then weight it until cold. Meanwhile remove any fat from the top of the stock and then pour this over and around the galantine when cool and chill until it jellies. Serve cold cut into slices with a salad and jacket potatoes.

Osso Buco

Ingredients (serves 3–4)
6–8 shin of veal bones sawn into
   5 cm (2 in) pieces with plenty of
   meat around
3 tablespoons oil
1 medium onion, sliced
150 ml (¼ pint) white wine
2 cloves garlic, chopped
450 g (1 lb) peeled tomatoes

300 ml (½ pint) white stock
salt and pepper

To garnish
1 large lemon
4 tablespoons chopped parsley
1 garlic clove

Turn the cooker to HIGH for 20 minutes. See that the shin bones have plenty of marrow. Heat the oil and quickly fry them, seeing that the marrow does not spill out, then add the onion and soften it. Pour the wine around and let it bubble for about 5 minutes. Transfer to the cooker and add all other ingredients except the garnish, seasoning well. Cover and cook for half an hour on HIGH, then on LOW for 6–8 hours.

Meanwhile grate the peel of the lemon very finely and mix it well with the chopped parsley, and the chopped garlic clove. Put this mixture (known as *gremolata* in Italy) on top, 10 minutes before serving. Traditionally this is served with *Risotto Milanese*, page 115.

Veal with Ratatouille

(Serves 4)
Prepare the *Ratatouille* given on page 114, and before cooking add 675 g (1½ lb) chopped veal, either from the shoulder or breast, which has been quickly turned in oil, then sprinkle with flour. Turn the cooker to HIGH for 20 minutes, mix the veal with the other sautéed vegetables, and when hot transfer to the cooker. Then cook on LOW for 8 hours.

Veal Brawn

This can be made with cooked leftover veal and ham or bacon, in which case reduce cooking time by 2 hours.

Ingredients (serves 4–6)
450 g (1 lb) any cheap cut veal
450 g (1 lb) lean boiling bacon
1 tablespoon chopped, mixed
   parsley, lovage, or tarragon

3 hard-boiled eggs
salt and freshly ground white
   pepper
approximately 300 ml (½ pint)
   stock or water

Turn the cooker to HIGH for 20 minutes. Lightly grease a basin to fit cooker. Mince or chop the meats and add the chopped herbs, salt and pepper. Slice the hard-boiled eggs thickly, then put alternate layers of meat and egg in the basin, ending with a layer of meat. Fill up with white stock or water, cover with foil, then put into the cooker and pour boiling water to half-way up the side of the basin. Cover and cook at HIGH for half an hour, then on LOW for 4–6 hours. Serve cold, cut into wedges, with a salad.

See also *Courgettes and Chicken*, page 36, *Stuffed Chicken Breasts*, page 51.

OFFAL

The slow cooker makes good meals from many of the less expensive kinds of liver, kidneys, hearts, oxtail, tongue and tripe for it develops the flavour and makes them tender and succulent.

Stuffed, Braised Lamb's Hearts

Ingredients (serves 4–6)
6 lamb's hearts
100 g (4 oz) made-up parsley and thyme stuffing, or use your own favourite recipe
1 heaped tablespoon seasoned flour
2–3 tablespoons oil
2 celery stalks, chopped
1 medium onion, sliced
450 ml (¾ pint) beef stock
1 bayleaf
pinch of mace and ground marjoram
salt and freshly ground pepper

Turn the cooker to HIGH for 20 minutes. Wash and clean the hearts thoroughly and remove any fat, pipes or bits of gristle. Make an incision down one side so that it forms a 'pocket' for the stuffing, then fill them and secure with skewers. Roll them in seasoned flour. Heat the oil and just soften the onion and celery in it, and put them in the cooker. Fry the hearts quickly all over and pour the stock over and add the herbs and seasoning. When boiling put into the cooker. Cover and cook on HIGH for half an hour, then on LOW for 8–10 hours, or HIGH for 4–5 hours.

Variations
1 Add a medium-sized can of tomatoes mixed with a pinch of basil and seasoned, and reduce stock to 300 ml (½ pint).

2 Stuff with seasoned sausagemeat and add a can of baked beans to the braise half an hour before serving and cook on HIGH to heat them through.

Cheap Kidney Casserole

The cheapest kidneys come from the ox but pig's or lamb's kidneys can also be used.

Ingredients (serves 4)
1 large ox kidney or 4 pig's kidneys
2 tablespoons seasoned flour
1 large onion, sliced
300 ml (½ pint) beef stock or half
  red wine and stock

salt and pepper
1 tablespoon chopped parsley
a pinch ground marjoram

Turn the cooker to HIGH for 20 minutes. Skin the kidney, cut in half and after taking out the central piece of fat, roll it in seasoned flour. Put into the cooker with the chopped onion herbs, and seasoning. Heat the stock and pour over. Cover and cook on HIGH for half an hour, then cook on LOW for 6–8 hours, or HIGH for 3–4 hours.

Variation Add 2–3 rashers of bacon cut into pieces and browned first, then 1 hour before it is ready add 100 g (4 oz) sliced mushrooms, pushing them down into the liquid.

LIVER

There are five different kinds of liver – lamb's, calf's, pig's, ox and chicken – generally available. Personally I think lamb's liver is best quickly fried, but all the others can be cooked to advantage in the slow cooker, and used in any of the following recipes.

Liver Casserole

Use the recipe above for *Kidney Casserole*, but first roll the liver in flour and quickly seal in a little hot oil before putting in the cooker.

Braised Liver and Onions

Ingredients (serves 4)
2–3 tablespoons oil
2 large onions, sliced
450 g (1 lb) calf's, ox or pig's liver
1 tablespoon seasoned flour

450 ml (¾ pint) beef stock
½ teaspoon powdered marjoram
1 bayleaf
salt and pepper

Turn the cooker to HIGH for 20 minutes. Heat the oil and just soften the onions in it, then put into the cooker. Coat the liver in the flour and seal it in the pan. Add the herbs and stock. Bring to boil and transfer to cooker. Cover and cook on HIGH for half an hour, then on LOW for 4–6 hours.

Pig's Liver Casserole

Ingredients (*serves 4*)
450 g (1 lb) pig's liver
seasoned flour
1 large onion, thinly sliced
6 rashers streaky bacon

1 tablespoon chopped parsley
salt and pepper
approximately 450 ml (¾ pint) beef
  stock

Turn the cooker to HIGH for 20 minutes. Roll the slices of liver in
the flour. Take the rind from the bacon. Put a layer of onion at the
bottom of the cooker, then one of liver and parsley, then top with
bacon, and repeat this until all is used. Heat the stock and pour
over, seasoning to taste. Cover and cook on HIGH for half an hour,
then on LOW for 4–6 hours, or HIGH for 2–3 hours.

See also *Chicken Liver Pâté*, page 43.

Braised Oxtail

It is best to cook oxtail the day before eating it, so that all fat can
be removed from the top before reheating, but remove it from cooker
to cool.

Ingredients (*serves about 4*)
1 oxtail, about 1 kg (2¼ lb), jointed
2 tablespoons oil
1 large onion, sliced
1 tablespoon tomato purée
1 bayleaf

1 tablespoon flour
½ teaspoon powdered marjoram
450 ml (¾ pint) beef stock
150 ml (¼ pint) red wine
salt and pepper

Turn the cooker to HIGH for 20 minutes. Trim the oxtail of as
much fat as possible before starting to cook. Heat the oil and soften
the onion in it and put into the cooker. In the same oil turn the
oxtail so that it browns all over. Add the tomato purée, bayleaf and
flour, and let it cook for about 1 minute. Then add all the other
ingredients, cover and cook on HIGH for 30 minutes, then on LOW
for 10–12 hours, or HIGH for 5–6 hours.

Variation Add 225 g (½ lb) chopped ox kidney, after sautéeing it in
the oil. This makes a very succulent braise.

TONGUE

Calf or ox tongue cooks beautifully in the slow cooker, as it keeps
its shape and there is no shrinkage. Trim it first of gristle, fat or
horny pieces of bone before soaking it overnight, if pickled.

Then curl it round the bottom of the cooker, add 1 onion, sliced, a bayleaf, some peppercorns and enough hot water (about 1 litre or 2 pints) to cover it. Put the lid on, cook on HIGH for 2 hours, then on LOW overnight or for 8–10 hours. Leave to cool in the liquid. Serve either cold or hot, and if the latter use either a *Sweet-sour Sauce*, see page 107, or the following *Polish Sauce*.

Polish Sauce

For tongue or ham.

Ingredients

1 tablespoon butter or margarine
1 heaped tablespoon flour
peel and juice of 1 lemon
1 tablespoon tarragon vinegar
1 tablespoon brown sugar
300 ml (½ pint) tongue stock (taste for saltiness)
300 ml (½ pint) sweet white wine
50 g (2 oz) sultanas
2 tablespoons blanched and split almonds
pinch of cinnamon

Melt the butter and add the flour, letting it cook for 1 minute. Pour in the warm stock, stirring to avoid lumps. Add the wine and all other ingredients, stirring well after each addition. Serve hot over the tongue slices.

Lamb's Tongues

They can be cooked as above but will only need cooking for 30 minutes on HIGH, then on LOW for 8–10 hours or HIGH for 4–5 hours. Serve with either of the above sauces, hot, or with a parsley sauce.

Tripe Lyonnaise

Ingredients (serves 4)

450 g (1 lb) dressed tripe
2 tablespoons oil
2 medium onions, sliced
1 clove garlic, chopped
1 green pepper, sliced (optional)
1 bayleaf
salt and pepper
300 ml (½ pint) tomato juice
300 ml (½ pint) chicken stock
1 tablespoon chopped parsley
125 g (4 oz) mushrooms
1 tablespoon cornflour

Turn the cooker to HIGH for 20 minutes. Cut the tripe into serving pieces. Place in a saucepan, cover with water, bring to the boil and throw the water away. Pat it dry. Heat the oil and lightly fry the onions, garlic, pepper, bayleaf and tripe for a few minutes. Season, and add the stock and tomato juice. Bring to the boil, add the parsley and the sliced mushrooms, then transfer to the cooker, cover and cook on HIGH for 30 minutes, then on LOW for 8–10 hours, or HIGH for 4–5 hours. Test the tripe for tenderness before serving or thickening. When ready, cream the cornflour with a little water, turn cooker to HIGH, add the cornflour, stir, and heat until it thickens.

See also *Philadelphia Pepperpot*, page 19.

Sauces

Many different kinds of sauces can be made in the crockery pot slow cooker, and will not diminish by evaporation in cooking. It is a good idea to make up a large quantity and then if you have a freezer it can be frozen in amounts you are most likely to use: remembering to leave about 2.5 cm (1 in) headspace in the container to allow for expansion.

Large quantities of sauce are also useful when serving pasta or rice to a number of people for a party. Double the quantities if you have the large crock-pot, and make the sauce, keep it hot on LOW, then serve over the cooked pasta or rice.

I have also included a cheese fondue in this chapter, for basically it is a sauce served with bread. The slow cooker is perfect for fondue parties: the heat is even, the bowl capacious and there is no likelihood of the fuel running out.

Barbecue Sauce (2)
This is a good sauce for serving with grilled or baked spare ribs; pork chops, roast chicken, sausages, hamburgers, etc.

Ingredients

450 g (1 lb) peeled, chopped tomatoes
1 medium onion, finely chopped
1 clove garlic, chopped
1 tablespoon brown sugar
1 tablespoon butter or margarine
salt and pepper

3 tablespoons Worcestershire sauce
150 ml (¼ pint) wine vinegar
2 teaspoons celery seed
¼ teaspoon dry mustard powder
4 tablespoons tomato pickle or chutney
pinch of cayenne pepper

Turn the cooker to HIGH for 20 minutes. Combine all ingredients, seeing that the tomatoes are chopped well, and mix thoroughly. Cover and cook on LOW for 3–4 hours.

Makes about 1–1.25 litres (1½–2 pints) sauce.

Bolognese Sauce

This is the famous Italian sauce for serving with cooked, dried beans, or pasta and it is also used in *Lasagne*, page 116, and cannelloni. There are many inferior imitations of this sauce which, when made with the correct ingredients, is really superb.

Ingredients
1 tablespoon oil or butter
100 g (4 oz) lean and fat bacon, chopped
2 medium onions, finely chopped
450–675 g (1–1½ lb) lean, raw minced beef
4 chicken livers
salt and freshly ground pepper
100 g (4 oz) minced lean pork or veal
pinch of nutmeg
1 medium-size can tomatoes
1 teaspoon dried basil
300 ml (½ pint) stock or water
150 ml (¼ pint) white wine
2 tablespoons tomato purée

Turn the cooker to HIGH for 20 minutes. Heat the oil in a large frying pan and soften the bacon in it. Add the onion, the beef and then the chicken livers, pork or veal. Mix them well, and cook quickly, turning continually so that the meats brown all over. Season, then add the nutmeg, the tomatoes, roughly chopped, the basil, stock and wine. Mix well and when amalgamated stir in the tomato purée. Transfer to the cooker, cover and cook on HIGH for 30 minutes, then on LOW for 6–8 hours, or HIGH for 3–4 hours. Serve with pasta and grated hard cheese such as Parmesan.

Variation The above is not nursery fare, and a simpler, but not so good version, can be made by omitting the chicken livers and pork, increasing the stock and omitting the wine.

Chilli Sauce

This is not made from the very hot chillis: it is only mildly spiced and similar to a ketchup, and can be used in the same way. If kept airtight and in a cold place it will keep for some time.

Ingredients
1 large can tomatoes
6 tablespoons cider vinegar
2 teaspoons cornflour
1 medium onion, chopped
1 medium green pepper, chopped (optional)
1 teaspoon cinnamon
pinch of ground cloves
pinch of chilli powder or cayenne
¼ teaspoon ground allspice
2 teaspoons salt

Turn the cooker to HIGH for 20 minutes. Sieve or mash the tomatoes. Cream the cornflour with a little water and boil up with the vinegar and tomatoes. Add the onion, green pepper and all the spices and salt. Transfer to the cooker, cover and cook on HIGH for 30 minutes. then on LOW for 3–4 hours, or HIGH for 2 hours.

When cold, liquidize and bottle. Makes about 600 ml (1 pint)

Cranberry Sauce
For serving with pork, goose, duck or turkey.

Ingredients
450 g (1 lb) cranberries
225 g (½ lb) cooking apples, peeled and sliced
1 medium onion, sliced
2 tablespoons sugar
salt and pepper

300 ml (½ pint) dark beer, boiling
2 teaspoons wine vinegar
a pinch dry mustard
a pinch cinnamon
4 tablespoons brown stock, preferably giblet gravy
4 tablespoons fresh breadcrumbs

Turn the cooker to HIGH for 20 minutes. See that the apples are finely sliced, also the onion. Combine all ingredients in the cooker, adding the hot beer last. Stir, cover and cook on HIGH for 30 minutes, then on LOW for 3–4 hours or HIGH for 2 hours.

Makes about 1.25 litres (2 pints).

Creole Sauce
This is good with hot chicken, lamb, pork or veal or with seafood. Fillets of fish can be baked in it.

Ingredients
2 tablespoons oil
2 medium onions, sliced
2 small green peppers, sliced
100 g (4 oz) mushrooms, sliced
1 teaspoon dried basil

a few drops Tabasco sauce
1 medium clove garlic, chopped
2 tablespoons parsley, chopped
1 kg (2¼ lb) tomatoes, peeled and chopped
salt and pepper

Turn the cooker to HIGH for 20 minutes. Heat the oil and just soften the onion, green peppers and mushrooms. Then add all other ingredients, transfer to cooker, cover and cook on HIGH for 30 minutes, then on LOW for 4–6 hours, or HIGH for 2–4.
Makes about 1.25 litres (2 pints) sauce.

Curry Sauce
See *Chicken Curry*, page 37.

Espagnole or Spanish Sauce

This is an excellent sauce which can also be used as a basis for other sauces such as Madeira, Marsala, Robert and many others. It freezes very well.

Ingredients
100 g (4 oz) bacon, chopped
bouquet garni
100 g (4 oz) butter
1 medium onion, chopped
1 medium carrot, finely sliced
1 small leek, chopped
1 stalk celery, chopped

50 g (2 oz) plain flour
3 tablespoons tomato purée
1.25 litres (2 pints) brown stock, see page 12, or use canned consommé
salt and pepper
2–3 tablespoons sherry, optional

Turn the cooker to HIGH for 20 minutes. Heat a pan, melt the butter and add the bacon. Let the fat run out and add all the vegetables and the bouquet garni. Let them just soften not colour. Stir in the flour and let it cook for 1 minute, then the tomato purée, mixing well, and add the brown stock and seasoning. Let it boil, then transfer to the cooker, cover and cook on LOW for 6–8 hours or HIGH for 3–4 hours.

Strain when cooked, and thicken slightly with a *beurre manié* (a walnut of butter mixed with as much flavour as it will take) if necessary, then add the sherry and use as required. Makes about 1.5 litres (2½ pints).

Plum Sauce

This is a sauce from Cornwall and the West Country: it is delicious with baked or boiled ham, lamb or pork. Rhubarb can also be used, and dried, soaked apricots cooked in the same way are very good with ham or pork.

Ingredients
1 kg (2¼ lb) plums, stoned and halved
225 g (½ lb) sugar

2.5 cm (1 in) stick cinnamon
1 teaspoon mace or 2 small blades
pinch of ground cloves
½ teaspoon salt

Turn the cooker to HIGH for 20 minutes. Put all the ingredients into the cooker, cover and cook on HIGH for 30 minutes, then on LOW for 6–8 hours, or HIGH for 3–4 hours. When cool, liquidize.

Makes about 1.3 kg (3 lb) sauce.

Sweet-sour Sauce

See *Sweet-sour Chicken*, page 42.

The sauce given below is good with chicken, duck, pork or turkey.

Ingredients

4 medium onions, peeled and chopped

4 stalks celery, finely chopped

100 g (4 oz) brown sugar

2 teaspoons paprika

600 ml (1 pint) pineapple juice, hot

300 ml ($\frac{1}{2}$ pint) white vinegar, hot

300 ml ($\frac{1}{2}$ pint) water, boiling

2 tablespoons honey

2–3 teaspoons soy sauce

2 tablespoons cornflour

Turn the cooker to HIGH for 20 minutes. Put all the ingredients except the cornflour into the cooker, cover and cook on HIGH for 30 minutes or until it is just simmering. Cook on HIGH for 3–4 hours, or LOW for 6–8 hours. When all vegetables are soft, liquidize. Heat the sauce to boiling, add the cornflour creamed with a little water, and stir until it thickens and is smooth.

Makes about 1.8 litres (3 pints).

See also *Dál Sauce*, page 16, *Tarragon Sauce*, page 41.

FONDUES

The slow cooker is very good for fondues; not only for making a cheese fondue, but also for making the sauce and keeping it at an even temperature for other fondues.

Bagna Cauda

This is a spicy sauce which comes from Piedmont in Italy. It does not mean 'hot bath' as it is often called, for it is Piedmontese dialect, simply meaning hot sauce. In a big saucepan heat 100 g (4 oz) butter with an equal amount of olive oil, then add 4 or 5 cloves garlic, but do not let them brown. Put in 6 anchovy fillets, chopped, and break them up until they disintegrate, stirring all the time.

Put this into the cooker and keep at LOW, then dip assorted and *crisp* vegetables into the sauce, such as pieces of celery, cauliflowerlets, quartered chicory, small chunks of white cabbage, radishes, sliced carrots, turnips, mushrooms and so on. But they must all be crisp, cold and raw.

Cheese Fondue

The timing of this is important, so do not let it go longer than the time given below.

Ingredients (serves 2–3)
1 clove garlic, halved
150 ml (¼ pint) dry white wine
225 g (½ lb) Gruyère or Blarney cheese, grated
225 g (½ lb) Emmenthal cheese, grated
1 tablespoon lemon juice
4 level teaspoons cornflour
pepper and pinch grated nutmeg

Rub the inside of the cooker all over with the garlic. Put the wine and lemon juice into the cooker and heat on LOW for 30 minutes. Mix the cheese with the cornflour and seasonings very well. Add this cheese mixture to the wine and stir thoroughly. Cover and cook on LOW for 1½ hours, stirring after half an hour. The fondue can be left on LOW in the cooker with the lid off, for 1–2 hours without spoiling.

To serve, leave in the cooker, and put bite-sized chunks of crusty bread on to a long fork and dip into the fondue. It is a good dish after being out in the open air on a cold day.

If it gets too thick, turn to HIGH and add 1 or 2 warmed tablespoons wine and stir until blended, then go back to LOW.

Fondue Dip

This is a good dip for a party, which will keep hot on LOW for several hours.

Ingredients (serves about 10)
225 g (½ lb) Cheddar cheese, grated
2 medium-size cans undiluted celery or asparagus soup
1 tablespoon Worcestershire sauce
a few drops Tabasco sauce
1 tablespoon chopped chives or green onion tops
1 tablespoon chopped parsley

Turn the cooker to HIGH for 20 minutes. Combine cheese, sauces and soup and mix well. Transfer to cooker, cover and cook on LOW for 2–3 hours. Stir to see that it is well blended, sprinkle with chives and parsley and keep on LOW while celery sticks, cauliflowerlets, chicory, etc., are dipped into the fondue.

See also *Bagna Cauda,* page 107, *Chocolate Fondue,* page 121.

Vegetables

Different types of vegetables require different methods of cooking in the crockery pot, but they all keep their flavour well, owing to the fact that there is only a little evaporation loss.

It is excellent for all members of the vegetable marrow family, and potatoes can be 'baked' without liquid in the cooker.

Root vegetables can take as long or longer to cook than meat, so follow instructions given below for cooking. Generally speaking they should all be cooked at HIGH unless used with meat, as long cooking on LOW can cause them to dry out and discolour.

Frozen vegetables cook more quickly if thawed, when they can be added to a dish about half an hour before they are needed.

Instructions for Cooking Vegetables

1 Always preheat the cooker to HIGH for 20 minutes.

2 Cook root vegetables on HIGH unless mixing with meat, etc., in a casserole dish.

3 Peel and slice all vegetables finely, and if possible keep them all to a similar size.

4 Root vegetables, even when cooked with other foods, should be put at the bottom of the cooker and covered with boiling water.

5 Dried beans and chick peas must be soaked overnight and cooked as for *Cassoulet*, page 90, omitting the tomato purée if needed for salads, etc.

Cabbage Rolls
See *Golubsty*, page 78.

Red Cabbage with Apples
Ingredients (serves 6–8)
2 tablespoons oil
2 tablespoons wine vinegar
3 rashers of bacon, diced (optional)

1 medium onion, finely chopped
1 medium red cabbage, shredded
 finely

Continued on next page

1 large cooking apple, peeled,
cored and sliced
150 ml (¼ pint) approximately
cider, wine or water

1 rounded tablespoon brown sugar
2 whole cloves and 2–3 whole
allspice
salt and pepper

Turn the cooker to HIGH for 20 minutes. Heat the oil in a large
saucepan, add the bacon and soften it, then put the onion in and
fry it very lightly. Add all the other ingredients and bring to the
boil. Transfer to the cooker, cover and cook on LOW for 8–10 hours.
Red cabbage cooked this way is excellent with pork or game.

Carrots

See *Root Vegetables*, above and page 114.

Cauliflower and Tomato Ragout

Ingredients (serves 3–4)
2–3 tablespoons oil
1 small onion, sliced
1–2 cloves garlic, pulped
150 ml (¼ pint) water or chicken
stock
450 g (1 lb) tomatoes, canned
1 medium cauliflower, cut into
flowerlets

100 g (¼ lb) cooked, or half-cooked
rice
pinch of dried basil
salt and pepper

To garnish
2 tablespoons chopped parsley

Turn the cooker to HIGH for 20 minutes. Heat the oil and lightly
fry the onion and garlic until soft, but not coloured. Add the
tomatoes, cauliflowerlets, basil, salt and pepper, and stock, and
bring to the boil. Layer with the rice in the cooker, cover and cook
on LOW for 6–8 hours. Garnish with the parsley.

Variation Pour over 600 ml (1 pint) cheese sauce when cooked,
and if using the removable pot type of cooker, brown under the
grill or in the oven.

Garnish with criss-crossed anchovies.

Jugged Celery

Ingredients (serves 4–6)
675 g (1½ lb) cooking apples
1 medium head of celery
4 whole cloves

4 rashers streaky bacon
1 tablespoon sugar
salt and pepper

Turn the cooker to HIGH for 20 minutes. Peel, core and slice the
apples and cook them with as little water as possible until they form
a stiff purée. Add the cloves and sugar and mix well. Wash and

trim the celery and cut it into thin strips, leaving them the height of the cooker if it is a deep one, or the width of the shallow pot. Chop the rashers and put half on the bottom, the apple purée on top and in an upright position (for the deep pot) stand as many sticks as the pot will hold. (Lay across for the shallow pot.) Season, put the rest of the bacon on top, cover and cook on LOW for 6–8 hours or HIGH for 3–4 hours.

Courgettes Niçoise

Ingredients (serves about 6)
450 g (1 lb) courgettes, sliced but not peeled
1 green or red pepper, seeded and sliced
1 medium onion, chopped
1–2 cloves garlic, crushed
225 g (½ lb) tomatoes, peeled and sliced

8–10 olives, black preferably
50 g (2 oz) butter
salt and butter

To garnish
2 tablespoons chopped parsley

Turn the cooker to HIGH for 20 minutes. Layer the courgettes, pepper, onion and garlic in the cooker, season, and put the sliced tomatoes and olives on top. Dot with the butter and cook on LOW for 6–8 hours or on HIGH for 3–4 hours. Garnish with the parsley.

Leek Hot-Pot

Ingredients (serves 4–5)
10 leeks, cut into 1 cm (½ in) rings
1 tablespoon butter or oil
150 ml (¼ pint) white wine or cider
150 ml (¼ pint) chicken stock

3 diced bacon rashers
2 tablespoons chopped parsley
salt and freshly ground pepper
to thicken: 2 teaspoons cornflour

Turn the cooker to HIGH for 20 minutes. Prepare the leeks. Heat the butter and just soften them in it (do not colour them) for about 2 minutes. Add the chopped bacon and let the fat run, and add the other ingredients, excepting half the parsley. Bring to the boil, transfer to the cooker, cover and cook on LOW for 6–8 hours. If you like the sauce thickened, then cream the cornflour with a little water, turn the cooker to HIGH, stir in and cook until it boils, about 10 minutes. Serve with the rest of the parsley on top.

Lentil Purée

This recipe is for the brown or dark green lentils. This is very good with lamb, duck or game. See also *Lentil Soup* (under *Split Pea*), page 18.

Ingredients (serves 4–6)
1 tablespoon butter or oil
2 streaky rashers bacon, chopped
2 medium onions, finely chopped
225 g (½ lb) brown lentils
1 stalk celery, if available, chopped

bouquet garni of herbs
600 ml (1 pint) meat stock, or use
  1 teaspoon Marmite dissolved in
  water
salt and pepper

Turn the cooker to HIGH for 20 minutes. Heat the butter or oil, quickly fry the bacon and then add the onions and celery just to soften but not to colour. Add the lentils, bouquet garni and stock, let it boil, then transfer to the cooker and season. Cover and cook on HIGH for 30 minutes, then on LOW for 10–12 hours.

Note The orange Egyptian lentils will only require 4–6 hours on LOW.

Marrow Casserole

Ingredients (serves 4–6)
1 kg (2¼ lb) marrow, peeled and
  sliced
½ teaspoon salt
1 large sliced onion
225 g (½ lb) whole or sliced green
  beans, thaw if frozen

1 275 g (10 oz) can whole kernel corn
1 small can 200 g (7 oz)
  tomatoes
salt and pepper

Turn the cooker to HIGH for 20 minutes. Peel and slice the marrow and sprinkle with salt. Layer all ingredients in the cooker, seasoning as you go. Add the juice from the corn and the tomatoes, and make up with water if it does not just cover the vegetables. Cover and cook on HIGH for half an hour, then on LOW for 6–8 hours or HIGH for 3–4 hours.

Variation Add some chopped blanched bacon to the casserole and serve with grated cheese over each portion.

Baked Onions Stuffed with Cheese

Onions like the slow cooking of the crockery pot and can also be stuffed, making a very good light meal.

Ingredients (serves 3–4)
6–8 medium onions, peeled
150 g (5 oz) grated hard cheese
6 tablespoons fresh, white
  breadcrumbs

1 tablespoon chopped parsley
a pinch of marjoram
salt and freshly ground pepper
300 ml (½ pint) beef stock or
  consommé, boiling

Turn the cooker to HIGH for 20 minutes. Blanch the onions in boiling water for 2 minutes, drain and cool a little. Then take out the centres very carefully with an apple corer. Mix together the cheese, breadcrumbs, chopped onion centres, herbs and seasonings and fill the centre of the onions with this mixture, pressing down very well. Stand in the cooker side by side and pour the boiling stock or consommé over the top, damping the onions as you are doing it. Cover and cook on LOW for 6–8 hours or HIGH for 3–4 hours.

Variations

1 Omit the cheese and use a packet of stuffing made up, adding a little grated lemon peel.

2 Stuff with cooked mince, mixed with the onion centres and a pinch of mixed herbs.

Potatoes, Baked

See that the potatoes are all roughly the same medium size and free from blemishes. Wash them well and put into the cooker while still wet but do not add water. Cover and cook in the preheated cooker on LOW for 8–10 hours or until tender.

A second method is as follows: rub the potatoes all over with oil or fat, and proceed as above.

Potatoes, Boiled

New potatoes can be cooked in the following way: scrub them well, but do not peel or they may discolour. Put into the preheated cooker and barely cover with boiling water and salt. Cook on HIGH for 3–4 hours, testing at the minimum cooking time.

Scalloped Potatoes

Ingredients (serves 4–6)

1 kg (2¼ lb) peeled, sliced potatoes
50 g (2 oz) butter
100 g (4 oz) processed cheese slices
salt and pepper
1 garlic clove, crushed
300 ml (½ pint) cheese sauce (a sauce mix will do)

Turn the cooker to HIGH for 20 minutes. Slice the potatoes finely, soak in water for about 1 hour to loosen the starch, then drain and dry well. Grease the cooker with about half the butter, and put layers of potato, seasoning (not too much salt if the cheese is salty), garlic and cheese slices. Repeat this, ending with the potatoes. Melt the butter, and pour over before pouring the cheese sauce over the top, seeing that all the potatoes are covered. Put the lid on and cook on LOW for 4–6 hours.

Variations

1 This can be done with any of the sauce mixes, for example, mushroom, and add a few mushrooms; onion, and layer with some onions.

2 Use beef broth or consommé instead of the sauce, layering with cheese or vegetables.

See also *Scalloped Ham*, page 96.

Ratatouille

If you have the largest-size cooker, you can double these ingredients. Ratatouille freezes well, but make certain to leave 2.5 cm (1 in) headspace in the containers to allow for expansion. It is very good reheated when all the flavours have merged.

Ingredients (*serves 6–8*)	2 medium aubergines
3–4 tablespoons oil	4 medium courgettes, sliced
2 medium onions, chopped	6–8 coriander seeds
2 cloves garlic, chopped	salt and freshly ground pepper
2 green peppers, seeded and sliced	
450 g (1 lb) peeled and sliced tomatoes	

Turn the cooker to HIGH for 20 minutes. Heat the oil in a large pan and soften the onion, garlic and peppers. Meanwhile cut the aubergines into thick slices, put into a colander, salt them well for about half an hour, then rinse it under the cold tap and pat dry. Put all the vegetables into the pan, and if using fresh tomatoes add about 3 tablespoons hot water. Season well and add the coriander seeds. Transfer to the cooker, cover and cook on LOW for 8–10 hours, testing at the minimum time for tenderness.

Tian

This is a similar dish from Provence in France, and the name comes from the large dish which was used to cook it in the baker's oven, after the bread had been baked. Tian has a handful of spinach or chard leaves, chopped, and whatever other vegetables are in season. Leftover pieces of fish, poultry or meat are also added to make a good savoury stew.

ROOT VEGETABLES

All root vegetables must be finely sliced and completely covered by boiling liquid. They are best cooked on HIGH for about 3–4 hours.

Root Vegetable Casserole

Use a mixture of root vegetables, i.e. carrots, turnips, artichokes, parsnips with some onion and perhaps celery, all finely chopped. Cover with either good chicken stock, consommé, dissolved onion Oxo cubes, a diluted can of celery or other vegetable soup. Season and see that the liquid covers them completely. Cover and cook on HIGH for 3–4 hours, then sprinkle thickly with chopped parsley before serving. The stock or soup added acts like a sauce so the vegetables need not be strained.

See also *Bean Cassoulet*, page 90, *China Cholla*, page 81, *Cream of Corn Soup*, page 15, *Dál Soup*, page 16, *Split Pea Soup*, page 18, *Oatmeal and Leek Soup*, page 19, *Stuffed Courgettes, Sweet Peppers*, etc., page 81, for recipes using dried beans, peas, lentils and fresh vegetables.

RICE

As rice is an annual grass I have included it in this chapter. There are several recipes in the book using rice, such as *Arroz con Pollo*, page 33, *Turkish Chicken*, page 42, *Turkey Risotto*, page 53, *Rice Pudding*, page 126. Your favourite rice recipe can be adapted to slow cooking.

Risotto Milanese

If the saffron and beef bone marrow are omitted this becomes *Risotto Bianco*.

Ingredients (serves about 4)
25 g (1 oz) butter
1 tablespoon beef bone marrow
1 small onion, finely chopped
275 g (10 oz) long grain rice
a pinch of saffron, optional
4 tablespoons white wine

600 ml (1 pint) chicken stock or
    water, hot
salt and freshly ground pepper

To garnish
1 tablespoon butter and 1 of grated
    Parmesan cheese

Turn the cooker to HIGH for 20 minutes. In a large pan heat the butter and the beef bone marrow and fry the onion until soft, then add the rice and stir until it is well impregnated with the fat. Add the wine and let it be absorbed, then the saffron, seasoning and finally add the stock or water. Transfer to the cooker, stir well, cover and cook on LOW for 4–5 hours. One hour before serving stir again, check seasoning and if the rice seems to be a little dry add not more than about 3 tablespoons of stock or water.

Serve with a knob of butter on each portion and plenty of grated cheese. Risotto is traditionally eaten with *Osso Buco*, page 98, but it is extremely good as a dish on its own. Leftover pieces of meat or poultry can be added after the stock.

Risotto con Uova

This is a good and filling dish: it is made as above and served with hard-boiled eggs stuffed with cheese on the top.

PASTA

Pasta should be partly cooked before adding to the cooker, and in the case of lasagne cook the sheets for 10 minutes before using it. You can add any cooked pasta to a soup or stew, but add it toward the end of cooking time, so that it justs heats up and does not become mushy.

Lasagne

Cook the sheets of lasagne in plenty of salted boiling water for 10 minutes, then put into cold water. Butter the crockery pot, put a layer of pasta on the bottom, then a layer of *Sauce Bolognese*, page 104, then a layer of seasoned cooked spinach with a pinch of mace or nutmeg. Or use a layer of peeled sliced tomatoes if spinach is not available. Sprinkle each layer with grated hard cheese such as Parmesan, and season. Repeat this, ending with a layer of pasta. Cover with a cheese sauce.

Put the lid on and cook on LOW for 4–6 hours or HIGH for 2–3 hours. Serve with more grated cheese.

Note For the 2 litre (3¼ pint) cooker, the ingredients needed are 225 g (8 oz) raw lasagne pasta, *Sauce Bolognese* using 450 g (1 lb) meat, 600 ml (1 pint) cheese sauce, 225 g (½ lb) cooked spinach or raw tomatoes, and about 100 g (4 oz) grated cheese.

Macaroni Cheese

Cook 225 g (½ lb) macaroni for about 5 minutes in boiling salted water, and drain. Mix the macaroni with 600 ml (1 pint) cheese sauce (reserving half to put on top) and 3 tablespoons grated cheese, a pinch of dry mustard powder and pepper. While still hot add 1 beaten egg, mixing well. Put into the buttered preheated cooker, pour the rest of the sauce over the top and sprinkle with grated cheese. Cover and cook on LOW for 3–4 hours.

Sweet Dishes

Many kinds of sweet dishes cook very well in the crockery pot cooker, as it allows flavours to blend and it brings out the best of the fruits, spices, and so on. It is without peer for making custards: they never crack and are really as smooth as velvet. Likewise the rice pudding is 'like Mother or Grandmother used to make'. Also an important thing is that a hot pudding can be left on LOW until serving time.

Your favourite steamed pudding will cook away without any fear of the water boiling away, or taking up valuable space on the top of the stove. You can even cook your Christmas pudding this way providing your crockery pot cooker is of the deep kind.

An important point to remember is that you should find the correct-size basin or dish which will fit your cooker easily, so that the lid will sit properly. Keep it by you, and if shopping for one, then do measure the cooker before going out to avoid disappointment. Here are a variety of recipes for you to try, but experiment with your own recipes.

Baked Apples

Ingredients (serves 4)
4–6 cooking apples, roughly the same size
150 g (5 oz) mixed dried fruit
a pinch of ground cinnamon and cloves
75 g (3 oz) soft, brown sugar
150 ml ($\frac{1}{4}$ pint) boiling cider or water
a little butter

First grease the base of the cooker with the butter and turn to HIGH for 20 minutes.

Wash and core the apples, and fill with the mixture of fruit, spices and sugar. Arrange in the cooker and pour the hot liquid around. Cover and cook on LOW for 4–5 hours or HIGH for 2–3 hours.

Variations

1 Fill with mincemeat and proceed as above.

2 Fill with sugar mixed with 1 tablespoon ground almonds and 1 tablespoon chopped almonds.

3 Fill with dried fruits mixed with a little grated lemon or orange peel and mixed with 3–4 tablespoons of whipped cottage cheese.

4 Fill with crushed macaroons mixed with 2 tablespoons apricot jam or marmalade.

5 If using the lift-out cooker, the apples can be covered with a meringue mixture when cooked, and put into a low oven (170°C, 325°F, gas 3) for about 15 minutes or until the top is set and just peaking with brown.

Apple Butter

Also for plums or damsons with the stones removed.

This is an eighteenth-century preserve which is used with cakes, scones, for pie-filling or in other sweet dishes. If sterilized after making it will keep for months, but it will keep for weeks in a screw-top jar in the refrigerator. It can also be frozen, but leave an inch headspace to allow for expansion before covering.

Ingredients

12 unpeeled, medium-size cooking apples
600 ml (1 pint) cider
450 g (1 lb) sugar
1 teaspoon ground cinnamon
6 whole cloves
pinch ground allspice

Turn the cooker to HIGH for 20 minutes. Core and chop the apples and put them into the cooker with the cider. Cover and cook on HIGH for 2 hours, then on LOW for 6–8 hours or until the apples are mushy. Take them from the cooker and purée them in a food-mill. Put the puréed mixture back with the sugar and spices, cover and cook on LOW for 1–2 hours.

Then bottle, or leave until cold and freeze in containers. Makes about 1.5–2 kg (3–4 lb).

Apple Sauce

This is made the same way as Apple Butter, but the apples are first peeled and if a chunky apple sauce is wanted, do not put through the food-mill.

Apple Charlotte

This can be made with bread slices, breadcrumbs or even small bread cubes.

Ingredients (serves 4–6)
8 crustless slices of bread, either cubed, crumbed or left whole
100 g (4 oz) melted butter or margarine
225 g (½ lb) soft brown sugar

1 kg (2¼ lb) cooking apples, peeled, cored and chopped or use 4 cups apple sauce
pinch each of: ground nutmeg and cinnamon (not if using apple sauce above)

Turn the cooker to HIGH for 20 minutes. Mix the crumbs or cubes with the melted butter, reserving 2 tablespoons sugar and spices. If using whole slices, spread with butter and sprinkle the sugar and spices over the top. Grease the cooker and arrange alternate layers of bread and apple, ending with a layer of bread. Pour the remaining melted butter over the top, cover and cook on HIGH for 2–3 hours, or until apples are soft. It can be served hot or cold with cream or custard.

Variations

1 Use rhubarb instead of apple.

2 Use brown or rye breadcrumbs and toss them first in the melted butter with the spices, in a hot pan, then layer them with the apples. This is called *Danish Apple Cake*.

Apple Crunch

This can also be made with rhubarb.

Ingredients (serves 4–6)
6 medium cooking apples, peeled, cored and sliced
175 g (6 oz) brown sugar
3 tablespoons breadcrumbs or quick-cooking oatmeal
3 tablespoons brown sugar

100 g (4 oz) butter or margarine
pinch of cinnamon and nutmeg
2 tablespoons flour

To garnish
2–3 tablespoons bramble jelly

Turn the cooker to HIGH for 20 minutes. Grease it well and arrange the sliced apples in the bottom sprinkled with the sugar. Then mix all other ingredients together and put on top. Cover and cook on LOW for 6–8 hours, or HIGH for 3–4. When cool put blobs of bramble jelly on the top.

Apricot Upside-down Cake

If using the shallow lift-out cooker, then this cake can be made in it, but the deeper varieties, or fixed stoneware pot cooker will need a suitable dish or mould which will fit into the cooker easily.

Ingredients

2 tablespoons butter
100 g (4 oz) brown sugar
1 can apricots, 380 g (13½ oz) size
a few nuts or glacé cherries
   (optional)

For the sponge

100 g (4 oz) each of butter and
   castor sugar
2 large eggs
100 g (4 oz) sieved self-raising
   flour
approximately 2 tablespoons fruit
   juice

Turn the cooker to HIGH and put the butter in to melt. Then make the sponge by creaming the butter and sugar, and adding the beaten eggs, a little at a time, beating after each addition to get the air in. Fold in the flour with a metal spoon. The mixture should drop off the spoon easily; if it doesn't, add the apricot juice until it is the right consistency.

When the butter is melted, paint it around the sides of the basin or crockery pot, add the sugar and spread it evenly over the bottom. (Or you can dissolve it over the stove and then transfer to the cooker.) Arrange the fruits and/or nuts and cherries on the bottom and spread the sponge mixture evenly over the top. If using a separate dish, loosely cover with foil and the lid; pour boiling water to half-way up the basin and cook on HIGH for 1 hour, then on LOW for about 3 hours or on HIGH for 3 hours, or until firm.

Put a large plate over the top and invert the cake on to it, and serve warm or cold. See below if serving cold.

Variations

1 Use either peach or pineapple instead of apricot.

2 When cooked and inverted, pour over about 3–4 tablespoons of the remaining fruit juice, and the same of sherry. Leave to soak into the sponge for about 1 hour.

See also *Pears Hélène*, page 126.

Bread and Butter Pudding

Ingredients (serves 4)
8 large slices crustless white bread
50 g (2 oz) butter
3–4 tablespoons sultanas or raisins
juice and grated peel of 1 lemon
pinch of mixed spice
600 ml (1 pint) hot milk

2 tablespoons castor sugar
2 eggs

To garnish
brown sugar mixed with a good
  pinch cinnamon

Turn the cooker to HIGH for 20 minutes. Prepare a dish by lightly greasing it, if using the deeper crockery pot. Spread each bread slice with butter and put half into the greased crockery pot, butter side up. Add the dried fruit mixed with the lemon juice and grated peel, also the spice. Cover with the remaining bread, butter side upwards. Meanwhile heat the milk, dissolve the sugar in it and pour over the beaten eggs, stirring well. Pour this over the pudding and put a piece of foil or greaseproof paper on top. Then put the lid on and cook on LOW for 3–4 hours. Before serving, sprinkle the top with brown sugar mixed with a good pinch of cinnamon and let this melt. Or if using the lift-out pot type put under the grill or in the oven until it caramelizes, in about 5–10 minutes.

Variations

1 Omit the fruit and spread bread thickly with chunky marmalade, and add the juice and grated peel of an orange.

2 Just before serving either version, pour over 2–3 tablespoons rum.

Chocolate Fondue

This is good fun for a teenagers' party and it can also be made in larger quantities and stored for serving over ice-cream, in which case substitute a coffee liqueur for the coffee.

Ingredients (serves about 6)
175 g (6 oz) plain chocolate
100 g (4 oz) sugar
100 g (4 oz) butter
1 cup evaporated milk
3 tablespoons black coffee or a

coffee liqueur

To dip in the fondue
marshmallows, chunks of sponge
  cake, sponge fingers, banana
  chunks, etc.

Turn the cooker to HIGH for 20 minutes. Then add the chocolate broken up and heat on HIGH for about half an hour or until chocolate is melted. Stir in the sugar, butter and evaporated milk, mixing well. Cook on HIGH uncovered, stirring for about 10 minutes or until it is well mixed. Then add the coffee or liqueur, stirring continuously.

Turn to LOW and keep on LOW while dipping the foods into it on forks.

Chocolate Pudding

This needs a 1.5–2 litre (2½–3 pint) dish or mould. Halve the quantities for the smaller crockery pot.

Ingredients (serves 4–6)
225 g (½ lb) self-raising flour
50 g (2 oz) cocoa powder
100 g (4 oz) butter
100 g (4 oz) sugar
4 eggs
300 ml (½ pint) milk

100 g (4 oz) fresh breadcrumbs

To garnish
Cream, chocolate sauce, mocha
  icing, or Sharwood's Chocolate
  and Rum or Chocolate and Ginger
  sauce

Turn the cooker to HIGH and grease the dish well. Sift the flour and cocoa together. Cream the butter and sugar, beat the eggs and add gradually with a little of the flour mixture, each time beating well.

Add the milk with the remaining flour alternately, and finally fold in the breadcrumbs. Put the mixture into the basin. Put a trivet, upturned jam jar lid or upturned saucer in the cooker and cover the pudding with about 4 paper napkins to absorb any moisture. Put the lid on and cook on HIGH for 3–4 hours.

Serve warm or cold with one or other of the garnishes.

Chocolate and Ginger Pudding

This recipe requires a 1 litre (2 pint) dish if not cooking directly in the shallow crockery pot.

Ingredients (serves 4–6)
175 g (6 oz) soft butter or margarine
175 g (6 oz) soft brown sugar
2 large eggs or 3 smaller ones
2 tablespoons cocoa powder
150 g (5 oz) self-raising flour
2 level teaspoons baking powder

1 rounded teaspoon ground ginger
1 tablespoon chopped preserved
  ginger
4 tablespoons golden syrup or
  treacle
2 tablespoons orange juice

Turn the cooker to HIGH and grease the crockery pot or dish. Put the butter, sugar, eggs, cocoa powder, baking powder, flour and ground ginger into a bowl and beat thoroughly until smooth. Then add the chopped ginger and pour into the dish or crockery pot. If using a dish stand it on a trivet or jam jar lid and cover the top with about 4 paper napkins. Put the lid on and cook on HIGH for 3–4 hours. Test at minimum cooking time.

When cooked and cooled slightly, pour over the golden syrup or treacle, which has been heated but not boiled, with the orange juice. Serve warm.

Baked Custard

This is for the 3–3½ litre (4–6 pint) crockery pot. For the 2 litre (3¼ pint) cooker, halve the quantities.

Ingredients (serves 4–6)
4 eggs
25 g (1 oz) castor sugar, or to taste, vanilla sugar if possible
a few drops vanilla essence if vanilla sugar is not available

600 ml (1 pint) milk
nutmeg (optional)
a buttered 1 litre (1½ pint) soufflé dish or mould: or use 4–6 individual pots

Turn the cooker to HIGH for 20 minutes. Blend the eggs and sugar (with the vanilla essence) together well. Warm the milk until hot but not boiling and pour over the egg mixture, stirring all the time. Strain into the dish, sprinkle a little ground nutmeg over the top and then cover with foil.

Stand in the cooker and pour in enough boiling water to come half-way up the sides of the dish. Cover and cook on LOW 3–4 hours, or until a knife inserted in the centre comes out clean. Take from the cooker when done and chill thoroughly.

Caramel Custard (*Crème Caramel*)

Heat up 75 g (3 oz) sugar with 3 tablespoons water, let the sugar dissolve over a steady heat, but as soon as it dissolves do not stir and boil until it becomes a golden brown. When it has reached the colour you like, add 1 tablespoon cold water to prevent it getting darker. Stir and pour this evenly into a buttered mould, and pour the custard mixture over the top. Then cook as above.

Orange Custards with Caramel Sauce

(*To serve 6*)

Whisk 4 eggs with 25–50 g (1–2 oz) sugar, the grated rind of 1 orange, then pour over 300 ml (½ pint) of hot milk and the same of light cream. Taste for sweetness and pour into the dish or dishes, cover with foil and proceed as for *Custard* (above), but increase cooking time to LOW for 6–8 hours.

When cooked and cool, make a syrup with 100 g (4 oz) granulated sugar with the juice from the orange, boiling it until the sugar turns golden. Take off the heat and spoon over the custard and leave to cool.

Lemon can be used instead of orange if preferred.

Variation Put 2 tablespoons apricot jam in the bottom, pour the custard over and when cooked garnish with cream and grated plain chocolate.

Hot Fruit Salad

This is an unusual sweet and will be perfectly all right if kept at LOW for at least 1 hour while serving straight from the crockery pot. Turn the cooker to HIGH for 20 minutes. For 1 kg (2¼ lb) mixed fresh fruits make a syrup consisting of 600 ml (1 pint) cider or water and 225 g (½ lb) sugar, 2.5 cm (1 in) piece of cinnamon bark, 4–6 coriander seeds and 1 bayleaf. Boil this up and stir until the sugar is dissolved, then simmer for 15 minutes. Strain and keep hot.

Prepare a mixture of whatever fruit is in season, such as apricots, pears, plums, gooseberries, oranges, etc. seeing that both skin and stones are removed. Put the fruit into the heated cooker, then pour over the boiling syrup, cover and cook on LOW for at least 2 hours and up to 4 hours depending on which fruits are being cooked, or on HIGH for 1–2 hours.

Before serving pour over a little rum, brandy, sherry, or an orange liqueur such as Grand Marnier on special occasions.

Poached Fruit

All fruits can be cooked as above and served cold. Rhubarb cooks very well without breaking up in the crockery pot and is very good if the rind of 1 large orange with the juice is added to every 500 g (1 lb) of fruit, using less water.

Rhubarb is also delicious cooked with 1 or 2 tablespoons of redcurrant jelly and cider, but do not use more than about 150 ml (¼ pint) liquid to every 225 g (½ lb) of fruit as rhubarb makes a lot of juice.

Different fruits will need slight variations in the amount of liquid, but it is better to err on the scant side rather than the generous, for a little can always be added.

DRIED FRUITS

All dried fruits cook well in the crockery pot, and should be soaked for a few hours, either in water, cider or wine to cover, according to taste. Add a quarter of a lemon and a small stick of cinnamon (remove when cooked) to each 500 g (1 lb) fruit.

Cook on HIGH for 4 hours in a preheated cooker, or LOW for 6–8 hours.

Prunes with small pieces of preserved ginger, cooked in cider as above, are delicious.

Lemon Pudding

This is a pleasant hot pudding with a spongy top and a creamy-lemony custard underneath. Choose a soufflé dish about 1 litre (2 pints) in capacity which will fit easily into your cooker, and also a small trivet or jam jar lid.

Ingredients (*serves 4*)
2 large eggs
1½ tablespoons butter
50 g (2 oz) sugar
finely grated rind and juice of 1
  large lemon
3 tablespoons sifted flour
600 ml (1 pint) milk
icing sugar to garnish

Turn the cooker to HIGH for 20 minutes. Separate the whites from the yolks of the eggs. Lightly grease the dish and cream the rest of the butter with the sugar. Add the yolks, the grated rind and juice of the lemon, and then the flour. Beat this well, then gradually work in the milk and finally fold in the stiffly beaten egg whites. Pour this into the dish, seeing that it only comes to two-thirds of the way up. Cover with foil, stand on a trivet, then pour boiling water to half-way up. Put the lid on, and cook at HIGH for 3 hours. Sprinkle with icing sugar before serving, hot.

Variations Use orange instead of lemon.
Or, soft fruits such as raspberries, blackberries or strawberries can be added to the bottom of the dish before pouring the mixture into it.

Pears in Wine

Red wine is usually used for pears, but rosé gives a very delicate flavour, especially if a little grated lemon peel is added.

Peel the pears (about 6 medium size fit into most cookers) leaving them whole, with the stalks intact if possible. Heat about 450 ml (¾ pint) wine with about 100 g (4 oz) sugar, or according to taste, the lemon rind, until the sugar dissolves, then bring to a simmer. Arrange the pears, stalks up and pour the hot wine over them. Cover and cook on LOW for 4–6 hours. Turn the pears from time to time to let them colour and absorb the syrup.

Variations

1 Remove the cores with an apple corer and fill with redcurrant jelly before cooking; or a mixture of redcurrant jelly and crushed macaroons.

2 Remove from the wine syrup when cool and roll in grated coconut and serve with the syrup reduced to half by rapid boiling, around the base. These are known as *Pears Alma*.

Pears Hélène

See *Apricot Upside-down Cake*, page 120, but substitute cooked halved pears for the apricots at the bottom; also add 1 heaped tablespoon cocoa mixed with 2 tablespoons boiling water, and when it is cool add to the sponge mixture.

Macaroon Pear Crunch

Ingredients (serves 4–6)
4–6 fresh pears, peeled and cored
65 g (2½ oz) raisins or sultanas
2 tablespoons brown sugar
juice and grated rind of 1 lemon
150 ml (¼ pint) sweet white wine or cider, boiling
4 tablespoons medium sherry, boiling
6 macaroons, medium size

Turn the cooker to HIGH for 20 minutes. Peel, core and thinly slice the pears. Mix the dried fruit with the sugar, lemon rind and juice. Put alternate layers of pears and the dried fruit mixture in the cooker, pour the wines over and cook on LOW for 4–6 hours. When cold spoon into serving dish or dishes, crush the macaroons and spread them evenly over the top.

Rice Pudding

The slow cooking really does make it like the old-fashioned creamy rice pudding of long ago. Sago or tapioca can be cooked the same way.

Ingredients (serves 4–6)
75 g (3 oz) short grain rice
600 ml (1 pint) milk
150 ml (¼ pint) evaporated milk

50 g (2 oz) sugar	ground nutmeg
a knob of butter	

Lightly butter the inside of the cooker and turn it to HIGH for 20 minutes.

Put all ingredients except the butter and nutmeg into a saucepan and bring slowly to the boil, stirring all the time. Pour into the cooker, dot with the remaining butter and sprinkle with ground nutmeg. Cover and cook on LOW for 4–6 hours.

Double quantities can be made in the larger crockery pots and the cooking time will be approximately the same.

Variations

1 Add the finely grated rind of either an orange or lemon, and omit the nutmeg.

2 Add about 3–4 tablespoons sultanas before cooking.

STEAMED PUDDINGS

All kinds of steamed puddings can be cooked in the crockery pot in a basin. Use your favourite recipes and you will be delighted with the results, also the steam-free kitchen. It is perfect for Christmas Pudding as well, but the size will depend on your cooker size.

Christmas Pudding

Use your own recipe to fit a 1 litre (2 pint) basin which should fit comfortably into the cooker. Preheat the cooker to HIGH for 20 minutes and grease the basin. Then put the mixture into it, cover with foil, put into the cooker and pour boiling water to come two-thirds up the sides. Cover and cook on HIGH for 3 hours, then switch to LOW and cook for 18 hours. Let it get cold, then re-cover with greaseproof paper and fresh foil, and store in a cool place.

To reheat: cook for 30 minutes on HIGH then switch to LOW for 4½ hours, seeing that boiling water comes to at least half-way up the sides.

Canary Pudding

Ingredients (serves 3–4)

100 g (4 oz) butter or margarine	125 g (5 oz) self-raising flour
100 g (4 oz) castor sugar	2 standard eggs
	grated rind and juice of 1 lemon

Turn the cooker to HIGH for 20 minutes. Cream the butter and sugar together, beating very well. Then beat the eggs and add them with a spoonful of flour. Fold in the rest of the flour adding a very little milk if the mixture seems too stiff. It should be of dropping consistency.

Lightly grease a 600 ml (1 pint) basin and pour the mixture into it, or use 6 dariole moulds. Cover with foil, put into the cooker and pour boiling water to half-way up the basin. Put the lid on, and cook on HIGH for 3–4 hours for the large pudding, or 2–3 hours for the small ones.

The above is the basic mixture for light steamed puddings. If put into small moulds with raspberry jam in the bottom and sprinkled with grated coconut when cooked, they are called *Castle Puddings*.

Syrup Pudding 100 g (4 oz) of golden syrup is put into the bottom of the basin.

Ginger Pudding Add 1 rounded teaspoon ground ginger.

Spotted Dick Add 75 g (3 oz) dried fruits.

Chopped dates, figs, chopped peel and marmalade are all well-known additions, and the puddings take their name from the extra ingredient added.

Steamed Puddings

Steamed puddings can also be made with breadcrumbs as well as flour, and suet instead of butter or margarine. This is a basic recipe to fill a 600 ml (1 pint) basin.

Ingredients (serves 4–6)
50 g (2 oz) self-raising flour
50 g (2 oz) white breadcrumbs
50 g (2 oz) grated suet
1 egg beaten

150 ml ($\frac{1}{4}$ pint) approximately, milk
spice, ginger or fruit to flavour
50 g (2 oz) sugar or 4 tablespoons golden syrup

Mix dry ingredients together, add the egg and enough milk to make a smooth dropping consistency. Then proceed as for *Canary Pudding*, page 127.

Tea Breads and Cakes

The crockery pot cooker makes very good tea breads and cakes, and of course cake mixes can be made up and cooked with the minimum amount of trouble.

It is important that you have moulds, cake tins, loaf tins, etc. that will fit your cooker easily, allow for rising and are not too difficult to get out when the cake or bread is cooked. Spring-sided pans, and even some empty coffee tins can also be used.

Read the following instructions before starting to bake

1 Always turn cooker to HIGH before starting to bake.

2 Cover and tie the baking tin with foil.

3 Stand tin or dish on a trivet, jam jar lid or upturned saucer, and if none of these are available then crumple up some foil to make a base. See below for cake mixes.

4 Pour boiling water around to provide steam. See recipes.

5 Do not remove the lid or foil during the first 2 hours of cooking. If you want to check that the bread or cake is cooked, test after that time with a thin skewer or cocktail stick, but if further cooking is needed do not delay in putting the foil and lid back.

6 *For Cake Mixes* The pan containing the cake mix can be put straight on to the cooker without a trivet and water is not required. To absorb extra moisture created by the cooker, instead of using foil, cover the top of the uncooked cake mixture with about 5 layers of paper towelling.

7 *Breads* can be made in a variety of pans: even a 1 kg (2 lb) empty coffee tin can be used as the shape adapts well to the crockery pot and equals a 1.8 litre (3 pint) mould. Small earthenware flower pots* make prettily shaped loaves, or use Pyrex, Pyrosil, etc.

---

* When using a new flower pot for the first time for baking, grease it well and bake empty in a hot oven once or twice to season it.

Banana Bread

Ingredients

75 g (3 oz) butter or margarine
100 g (4 oz) sugar
2 eggs, lightly beaten
150 g (6 oz) flour
1 teaspoon baking powder
pinch of salt
3–4 ripe, mashed bananas,
   approximately 1 cup

Turn the cooker to HIGH for 20 minutes. Cream the butter and sugar together, add the eggs and beat well. Add the sifted flour and baking powder, alternately with a little banana, beating well after each addition. Pour into the well-greased container, cover with foil and tie down. Put on a trivet and cook on HIGH for 2–3 hours.

Variation Add 50 g (2 oz) chopped or glacé cherries. The bread can be served warm or cold and is particularly good if iced with cream or cottage cheese.

Cream Cheese Icing

Mix 4 tablespoons cottage or cream cheese with 125 g (5 oz) sieved icing sugar and 1 lightly beaten egg white.

Or the Banana Bread can be cut into slices and spread with cottage or cream cheese.

Boston Brown Bread

This is a traditional American bread, shaped in a round similar to a 450 g (1 lb) can and it is steamed not baked, so adapts well to the crockery pot.

Ingredients

125 g (5 oz) rye flour or plain white
   flour
125 g (5 oz) fine corn meal
125 g (5 oz) whole wheat flour
1 teaspoon salt
1 rounded teaspoon bicarbonate
   of soda
150 g (6 oz) dark treacle,
   approximately ¾ cup
600 ml (1 pint) sour milk or
   buttermilk, or
2 small cartons plain yoghurt and
   one third water
100 g (4 oz) raisins or sultanas
   (optional)

Turn the cooker to HIGH for 20 minutes. Mix and sift all dry ingredients. Mix together the treacle and milk and add to the dry mixture gradually, seeing that it is well mixed, but do not overbeat. Add the raisins. Then spoon into the well-greased container, cover and tie securely, but do not fill more than two thirds to allow for expansion.

Put the container on to a trivet, and pour about 600 ml (1 pint) boiling water around. Put the lid on and cook on HIGH for 3–4 hours. Let it cool in the container out of the cooker.

Variation Indian Bread is made as above, but the ingredients are: 400 g (14 oz) whole wheat flour to 100 g (4 oz) corn meal, 2 teaspoons bicarbonate of soda, 100 g (4 oz) treacle, 450 ml (¾ pint) sweet milk. Mix and steam as for *Boston Brown Bread*.

Bran Bread

This is another American steamed bread.

Ingredients
225 g (½ lb) whole wheat flour
2 cups all-bran cereal
pinch of salt
1 rounded teaspoon bicarbonate of soda
100 g (4 oz) raisins (optional)

1 large egg, beaten
100 g (4 oz) treacle, approximately 1 cup
450 ml (¾ pint) sour milk, buttermilk or plain yoghurt mixed with water (⅔ yoghurt, ⅓ water)

Turn the cooker to HIGH for 20 minutes. Mix together the flour, bran, salt, bicarbonate of soda and fruit. Beat the egg, treacle and milk together and mix gradually into the dry ingredients, but do not overbeat. Pour into a well-greased and floured dish, cover with foil and tie, and put on a trivet in the cooker.

Pour 600 ml (1 pint) boiling water around, cover the cooker and cook on HIGH for 3–4 hours.

Carrot Cake

Like the *Banana Bread*, page 130, this is very good served spread with cottage or cream cheese, although it makes a sweet cake as well.

Ingredients
150 g (6 oz) plain flour
2 teaspoons baking powder
1 teaspoon ground cinnamon
100 g (4 oz) grated carrots
grated rind and juice 1 orange

100 g (4 oz) butter or margarine
150 g (5 oz) castor sugar
2 beaten eggs
100 g (4 oz) chopped nuts (optional)

These quantities will fit into a round cake tin about 12–15 cm (5–6 in) in diameter.

Turn the cooker to HIGH for 20 minutes. Sift the flour with the dry ingredients. Mix the grated carrots with the grated rind and juice of the orange. Cream the butter and sugar, then add the eggs one at a time. Beat in the carrot and orange mixture, and finally add the flour and nuts if using them.

Put into a lightly greased dish or tin, cover with foil and tie, and put on a trivet in the cooker. Pour about 600 ml (1 pint) boiling water around, cover and cook on HIGH for 3–4 hours. Take from the cooker when done, stand until slightly cooled, then loosen the edges and cool on a cake rack.

Honey Cake

Ingredients

100 g (4 oz) white flour
100 g (4 oz) rye flour, or use all white
1 teaspoon baking powder
1 teaspoon bicarbonate of soda
1 teaspoon salt
1 teaspoon ground cinnamon
1 teaspoon ground ginger
100 g (4 oz) liquid honey
1 egg lightly beaten
barely 300 ml ($\frac{1}{2}$ pint) milk

Turn the cooker to HIGH for 20 minutes. Sift all dry ingredients and mix well. Add the honey, egg and milk beaten together and beat well for about 10 minutes. Put into a well-greased dish, cover with foil and tie it down. Then stand on a trivet, pour about 600 ml (1 pint) boiling water around, cover and cook on HIGH for 3–4 hours.

Fruit Cake

Ingredients

225 g (8 oz) flour
1 teaspoon each of baking powder and ground cinnamon
pinch of ground nutmeg
pinch of ground allspice
3 standard eggs
2 tablespoons golden syrup
100 g (4 oz) sugar
125 g (5 oz) raisins or mixed with sultanas
100 g (4 oz) chopped nuts
100 g (4 oz) chopped glacé cherries

Turn the cooker to HIGH for 20 minutes and prepare cake tin by greasing and lightly flouring. Sift and mix all dry ingredients, fold in the fruit and cherries and mix in the golden syrup. Add the beaten eggs gradually, then put into the prepared tin. Cover with foil and stand on a trivet in the cooker. Add about 600 ml (1 pint) boiling water, cover and cook on HIGH for 3–4 hours.

Note Check after the first 1$\frac{1}{2}$ hours that the water has not run dry.

CAKE MIXES

Instructions for using cake mixes in the crockery pot cooker are on page 129.

Miscellaneous (Chutneys, Preserves, Jams Beverages and Punch)

CHUTNEY

The crockery pot makes delicious chutney, and I think its versatility has been shown in the preceding pages. Chutney and preserves seem to benefit from the slow cooking and can happily be making while you are out. The flavours are excellent and there is no loss from evaporation.

Apple Chutney
Gooseberries can also be used in place of apples.

Ingredients

1.35 kg (3 lb) cooking apples
2 large onions, finely chopped
1 kg (2¼ lb) brown sugar
2 teaspoons salt
225 g (8 oz) sultanas or raisins
½ teaspoon cayenne pepper
2 teaspoons dry mustard powder
pinch of ground ginger
450 ml (¾ pint) white malt vinegar

Turn the cooker to HIGH for 20 minutes. Peel, core and finely chop the apples and onions. Put all the ingredients into the coooker and mix well. Cover, and cook on HIGH for 1 hour, then on LOW for 8–10 hours, or overnight. When cooked pour into heated jars and cover at once.

Makes about 2 kg (4 lb) chutney.

Variations

Indian Chutney Add 1 tablespoon turmeric powder and 2 teaspoons curry paste or powder.

Tomato Chutney Use 1.35 kg (3 lb) green or red tomatoes instead of the apples. Add 1 finely chopped celery heart and 1 seeded and sliced green or red pepper. Reduce the sugar to 225 g (½ lb).

Date and Banana Chutney

This is a useful chutney which can be made at any time of year.

Ingredients
12 bananas, ripe and sliced
450 g (1 lb) finely chopped onions
450 g (1 lb) chopped dates
450 g (1 lb) black treacle

600 ml (1 pint) malt vinegar
2 teaspoons curry powder
  (optional)
1 teaspoon ground ginger
2 teaspoons salt

Turn the cooker to HIGH for 20 minutes. Peel and chop the bananas, onions and dates very finely. Then combine all ingredients in the cooker, stir well, cover and cook on HIGH for 1 hour, then on LOW for 8–10 hours or overnight. Pour into warmed jars and cover at once. Makes about 2 kg (4 lb) chutney.

Peach Chutney

Apricots or plums can also be used and it is good served with curries.

Ingredients
1 kg (2¼ lb) peaches, canned or
  fresh, diced
100 g (4 oz) raisins or sultanas
1 medium onion, chopped
2 cloves garlic, chopped

1 teaspoon each of ground ginger
  and cayenne pepper
100 g (4 oz) brown sugar (225 g or
  ½ lb if using fresh peaches)
juice and rind of 1 lemon
300 ml (½ pint) white vinegar

Turn the cooker to HIGH for 20 minutes. Combine all ingredients in cooker and mix well. Cover and cook on HIGH for 1 hour, then on LOW for 4–6 hours (8–10 hours if using fresh peaches). Then take off the lid and cook on HIGH for 1–2 hours. Makes 1.5–2 kg (3–4 lb) chutney.

Marrow Pickle

Ingredients
1 large vegetable marrow, about
  1 kg (2¼ lb)
salt
450 g (1 lb) onions, finely sliced
450 g (1 lb) apples, peeled, cored
  and sliced

450 g (1 lb) granulated sugar
1 teaspoon cayenne pepper
2 teaspoons mixed pickling spice,
  tied in a bag
600 ml (1 pint) white vinegar
2 tablespoons turmeric powder

Peel, seed and cut the marrow into small cubes, put it on to a large dish, sprinkle thickly with salt and leave to stand covered overnight. The next day drain off the liquid, rinse it under the tap and pat dry.

Turn the cooker to HIGH for 20 minutes. Put all ingredients into the cooker except the turmeric powder. Cover and cook on HIGH for 1 hour, then on LOW for 8–10 hours or overnight. Half an hour before it is ready stir in the turmeric, turn to HIGH and finish cooking. Pour into warmed jars and tie down. Makes about 3 kg (6 lb).

PRESERVES

Lemon Curd

Lemon curd makes beautifully in the slow cooker, but *do not cook longer than the stated time*. Orange can be used in place of lemon and an unusual curd is made from blackberries, see below.

Ingredients	4 standard eggs
100 g (4 oz) butter	a basin which will hold 1 litre
grated zest and juice of 4 lemons	(1¾ pints)
450 g (1 lb) castor sugar	

Turn the cooker to HIGH for 20 minutes. Melt the butter in a saucepan but do not let it foam. Add the grated zest, juice and sugar. Stir until dissolved over a gentle heat, and leave it to cool.

Beat the eggs lightly and stir into the mixture. Pour this into the basin and cover with foil. Stand it on a small trivet or jam jar lid and pour about 150 ml (¼ pint) of boiling water around. Cook on LOW for 3½–4½ hours. Pour into warmed jars and seal while hot.

Variation Use orange zest and juice instead of lemon and proceed as above.

Blackberry Curd

Simmer 450 g (1 lb) blackberries in water to barely cover until they are soft. Then drain through a sieve, reserving 150 ml (¼ pint) juice. Add the juice of 1 lemon and increase the sugar to 575 g (1¼ lb). Then proceed as for lemon curd.

JAMS

Jams can be made by first softening the fruits with the water in the slow cooker for 6–8 hours or overnight, and then putting them into a large saucepan with the sugar, brought slowly to the boil so the sugar dissolves, then boiled rapidly for about 7–10 minutes. Test for setting and bottle in warmed jars and tie down at once.

Marmalade

Ingredients
1 kg (2¼ lb) Seville oranges
1 lemon

300 ml (½ pint) boiling water
1.8 litres (3 pints) boiling water
2 kg (4½ lb) sugar

Turn the cooker to HIGH for 20 minutes. Squeeze the juice from the oranges and the lemon and put the pips and pith in a small saucepan with the 300 ml (½ pint) water and simmer for 1 hour. Chop the peel according to taste and put that in the cooker with 1.8 litres (3 pints) boiling water. Cover and cook on LOW for 8–10 hours or overnight. Turn out into a large saucepan, add the sugar and strained pip juice and heat gently until the sugar dissolves, then bring to a rolling boil and boil for about 10–15 minutes, or until setting point is reached. Leave to stand for 10–15 minutes so that the peel distributes itself evenly, then pot and cover. Makes about 2.5 kg (6 lb) marmalade.

Porridge

Ingredients (serves about 4)
100 g (4 oz) oatmeal

900 ml (1½ pints) water
½–1 teaspoon salt

First turn cooker to HIGH for 20 minutes. Bring water to boil in a saucepan, then sprinkle in the oatmeal, stirring all the time for about 1 minute. Add the salt and transfer to the cooker. Cover and cook on LOW overnight.

BEVERAGES
Tomato Juice

Ingredients
12 large ripe tomatoes (about
  1.5–2 kg or 3–4 lb)
2 teaspoons salt

1 tablespoon sugar
½ teaspoon freshly ground white
  pepper

Turn the cooker to HIGH for 20 minutes. Wash tomatoes and remove the cores; put them into the cooker with the salt, sugar and pepper. If more convenient for your cooker cut them in half. Cover and cook on LOW for 6–8 hours or until they are mushy and soft.

Take out and press through a vegetable mill or fine sieve. Taste again for seasoning and chill. Makes about 1.2 litres (2 pints) juice.

Mulled Cider
All crockery pots are ideal for making and serving hot drinks or

punch, for although the liquid keeps hot it never boils on LOW, thus preserving the alcoholic content.

Ingredients (for about 10 drinks)
2.5 litres (4 pints) dry cider
2 tablespoons sugar, or to taste
1 small stick cinnamon
5–6 whole cloves
4 tablespoons medium sherry
1 orange and 1 lemon, thinly sliced, but unpeeled

Turn the cooker to HIGH for 20 minutes. Put all ingredients into the cooker, turn to LOW, cover and heat for 2–5 hours.
Serve from the crockery pot. It will keep longer at LOW if required.

Bishop

This was a favourite eighteenth-century drink and popular with Dean Jonathan Swift, *c.* 1723.

> . . . Fine oranges,
> Well roasted, with the sugar and wine in a cup,
> They'll make a sweet Bishop when gentlefolks sup.

Ingredients (for about 12 drinks)
3 oranges, each stuck with 3–4 whole cloves
1 small stick cinnamon
2 blades mace
4 allspice berries
pinch of nutmeg
a small piece ginger root
300 ml (½ pint) boiling water
6 lumps sugar rubbed on lemon rind
2 bottles port or red wine

Put the oranges into a pan and bake in a hot oven for 30 minutes. Turn the cooker to HIGH meanwhile and when the oranges are ready put them into the cooker and add the rest of the ingredients. Mix well, then cover and cook at LOW for 2–3 hours. Serve hot from the cooker.

Mulled Wine

Ingredients (for about 12 drinks)
2 bottles red wine
300 ml (½ pint) water
150 g (6 oz) sugar, or to taste
2 small cinnamon sticks
1 level teaspoon nutmeg
1 orange and 1 lemon, thinly sliced, but unpeeled
4 tablespoons brandy, optional

Turn the cooker to HIGH while preparing ingredients. Then put them all into the cooker and heat on LOW for at least 2 hours before serving hot, but it can be left longer.

Mulled Claret

This is made with 1 or 2 bottles of claret, 1 or 2 wineglasses of port, sugar to taste, the rind of 1 lemon, 10 whole cloves and a pinch of grated nutmeg. A wine glass of curaçao added just before serving is delicious. Put all ingredients into the cooker and heat at LOW as for *Mulled Wine*, page 137.

PUNCH

The slow cooker makes beautiful punch, and you have no fears about it boiling away or losing its alcoholic content.

Brandy Punch

Ingredients (for about 10 large drinks)
225 g (½ lb) sugar
600 ml (1 pint) boiling water
6 whole cloves
zest and juice of 2 lemons

zest and juice of 2 oranges
1 bottle red wine
150 ml (¼ pint) brandy
1 dessertspoon Angostura bitters
1 orange and 1 lemon, thinly sliced, but unpeeled

Turn the cooker to HIGH for 20 minutes, then put in the sugar and boiling water and stir well. Let the sugar dissolve thoroughly, then add all ingredients except the brandy.

Heat on LOW for 3–4 hours and just before serving add the brandy and let it warm through.

Rum Punch

Ingredients (for about 20 drinks)
1 bottle rum, either dark or light, but not white rum
1 cup weak, milkless tea, China or Indian
1 cup fresh orange juice or fresh lime juice

150 g (6 oz) sugar
6 tablespoons boiling water
1 tablespoon Angostura bitters
nutmeg

Turn the cooker to HIGH for 20 minutes. Put all ingredients except the sugar, water and nutmeg into the cooker. Then dissolve the sugar in the water over a low heat, and add to the cooker. Cover, and heat at LOW for 2–4 hours. Serve hot, sprinkled with a little nutmeg.

Index

Apple
  Apple butter 118
  Apple Charlotte 119
  Apple chutney 133
  Apple crunch 119
  Apple sauce 118
  Baked apples 117–18
  Danish apple cake 119

Beans
  Bean cassoulet 90
  Beef with beans 65
Beef
  Beef and green ginger casserole
    68–9
  Beef and kidney stew or pie 71–2
  Beef and pepper casserole 74–5
  Beef curry 66
  Beef goulash soup 14
  Beef olives 72
  Beef with beans 65
  Beef with walnuts and orange 77
  Boeuf à la mode 63–4
  Boeuf bourguignonne 64
  Boeuf carbonnade flamande 65–6
  Boeuf en daube 67
  Boiled corned beef and dumplings
    66
  Braised beef with stuffed prunes 75
  Glazed corned beef 66–7
  Hawaiian beef 70
  Hungarian beef or goulash 69–70
  Japanese beef 70–71
  Mexican beef 77–8
  Polynesian beef 72–3
  Pot roast 73
  Potted beef 74
  Roman beef stew 69
  Sauerbraten 75
  Sicilian beef 76
  Stracotto 76
  Stuffed beef flank 67–8
  Swiss steak 77
Beurre manié 15, 106
Beverages
  Bishop 137
  Brandy punch 138
  Mulled cider 136–7
  Mulled claret 138
  Mulled wine 137
  Punch 138
  Rum punch 138
  Tomato juice 136
Brotchán Roy 19

Cabbage
  Cabbage leaves, stuffed 78
  Red cabbage with apples 109–10
Cake mixes 129
Cassoulet 90–91
Cauliflower and tomato ragout 110
Celery, jugged 110
Chicken
  Baked chicken 33–4
  Chicken and liver paste 44–5
  Chicken and pepper casserole 74–5
  Chicken and prawn gumbo 17–18
  Chicken cacciatora 34–5
  Chicken contadini 35–6
  Chicken curry 37–8
  Chicken with honey and almonds
    38–9
  Chicken with rice and vegetables 33
  Chinese chicken 35

Chicken *continued.*
  Coq au vin 43
  Country chicken casserole 36
  Courgettes and chicken 36–7
  'Hunter's' chicken 34–5
  Israeli chicken 39–40
  Paprika chicken 41–2
  Poached chicken 40
  Roast chicken 33–4
  Stuffed chicken breasts 51
  Sweet-sour chicken 42
  Turkish chicken 42–3
Chilli con carne 77–8
China cholla 81–2
Chutney
  Apple chutney 133
  Date and banana chutney 134
  Indian chutney 133
  Marrow pickle 134–5
  Peach chutney 134
  Tomato chutney 133
Cider
  Cod in cider 22–3
  Herrings in cider 26
  Mackerel in cider 26
  Mulled cider 136–7
  Prunes in cider 125
Cod
  Cod Creole 23
  Cod in cider 22–3
Cooking times 9–10
Coq au vin 43
Courgettes
  Courgettes and chicken 36–7
  Courgettes Niçoise 111
  Courgettes, stuffed 81
Cream cheese icing 130
Crockery pots, use and care of 7–10
Croûtons 18, 43, 64
Curry
  Beef curry 66
  Chicken curry 37–8
  Curried fish 24
  Curry sauce 38
  Curry soup 18

Dried fruits 125–6

Dublin coddle 82
Duck
  Baked duck 45
  Duck agrodolce 45–6
  Duck au vin 50
  Duck Korma 47–8
  Duck pâté 50
  Duck with gooseberry sauce 47
  Duck with honeyed apricot sauce 46–7
  Duck with Marsala wine 48
  Duck with orange, flambéed 48–9
  Duck with pineapple 49–50
  Duck with port 50
  Roast duck 45
Dumplings 14, 66

Feathered game 54–8; *and see* Partridge, Pheasant, etc
Fish
  Casserole of spiced fish 21–2
  Curried fish 24
  Fish chowder 16–17
  Fish soufflé 25
  and see Cod, Herrings, etc
Fondues
  Bagna cauda 107
  Cheese fondue 108
  Chocolate fondue 121–2
  Fondue dip 108
Frozen foods 9
Fruit syrup 124
Furred game 58–61; *and see* Hare, Rabbit, etc

Game
  Braised game with grapes 55
  Game pâté 60
Game birds, braised 54–5
Gliny *see* Guinea fowl
Golubtsy 78
Guinea fowl, roast and stuffed 50–51

Ham
  Boiled ham or bacon 94
  Ham and apricot hot-pot 94–5

Ham or bacon loaf 95
Irish ham loaf 95–6
Scalloped ham 96
Hare
  Hare pâté 59–60
  Jugged hare 58–9
Herrings
  Baked herrings 26
  Jamaica 'trouts' 27
  Herrings baked in tea 26–7
  Yorkshire herring pie 31

Irish stew 82

Jam-making 135

Kidney casserole 100

Lamb or mutton
  China cholla 81–2
  Irish stew 82
  Lamb and kidney wine casserole 83
  Lamb with apples and cider 83
  Lamb with lentils 84
  Lamb with spinach and yoghurt 84
  Lamb's hearts, stuffed and braised 99
  Lamb's tongues 102
  Leg of mutton à l'étuvée 85–6
  Norman lamb casserole 85
  Persian lamb 86
  Pilaff of lamb 86
  Rosemary spiced lamb 87
  Saffron lamb casserole 87
  Shanks of lamb, spiced 87–8
  Spanish lamb casserole 88
Lasagne 116
Leek hot-pot 111
Leftover food 8–10
Lentil purée 111–12
Liver
  Braised liver and onions 100
  Liver casserole 100
  Pig's liver casserole 101

Mackerel
  Backed mackerel 26
  Cape Cod mackerel 29

Jamaica 'trouts' 27
Mackerel baked in tea 26–7
Mackerel with gooseberries and fennel 28
Mackerel with orange 28–9
West Country baked mackerel 28
Marinade 58
Marmalade 136
Marrow
  Marrow casserole 112
  Marrow pickle 134–5
  Stuffed marrow 81
Meat, directions for roasting 62–3; and see Beef, Lamb, etc
Minced meat dishes
  Chilli con carne 77–8
  Golubtsy 78
  Meat ball casserole 79
  Meat loaf 79–80
  Moussaka 80–81
  Stuffed courgettes, marrow or peppers 81
  Turkish meat loaf 80

Offal 99–103; and see Kidney, Liver, etc
Onions, baked and stuffed with cheese 112–13
Osso buco 98

Partridge
  Partridge au vin 55
  Partridge with cabbage 55–6
  Partridge with red cabbage and cider 56
Pasta
  Lasagne 116
  Macaroni cheese 116
Pastry, shortcrust 71–2
Pâté
  Chicken liver pâté 43–4
  Duck pâté 50
  Game pâté 60
  Hare pâté 59–60
  Pâté of pork, French country style 91–2
Pears
  Macaroon pear crunch 126

Pears *continued*.
　Pears Alma 126
　Pears Hélène 126
　Pears in wine 125–6
Peppers, stuffed 81
Pheasant
　Pheasant casserole 57
　Pheasant with apple and onion
　　purée 56–7
Pigeons
　Pigeon casserole 57
　Pigeons stuffed with almonds,
　　apricots and raisins 58
Pilchards, West Country baked 28
Plaice, Indian 25–6
Pork
　Braised pork chops Savoy 89
　Braised stuffed pork steaks
　　(fillets) 89–90
　Cassoulet 90–91
　Directions for roasting pork,
　　general 63
　Elizabethan ragout of pork 93
　Mexican pork chops 91
　Pâté of pork, French country
　　style 91–2
　Persian pork *see* Persian Lamb
　Pork and pineapple 92
　Pork chops and corn casserole
　　92
　Pork pot roast with leeks 92
　Roast pork with honey and
　　cranberries 93
　Roast pork with orange 93–4
　Roast, stuffed pork steaks 90
Porridge 136
Potato topping 72
Potatoes, baked, boiled or
　scalloped 113–14
Poultry 32–54; *and see* Chicken,
　Duck
Preserves
　Blackberry curd 135
　Lemon curd 135
Prunes
　Prunes in cider 125
　Stuffed prunes 75

Puddings
　Basic recipe for steamed puddings
　　128
　Bread and butter pudding 121
　Canary pudding 127–8
　Castle puddings 128
　Chocolate pudding 122
　Chocolate and ginger pudding
　　122–3
　Christmas pudding 127
　Ginger pudding 128
　Lemon pudding 125
　Rice pudding 126–7
　Spotted Dick 128
　Syrup pudding 128

Rabbit
　Normandy rabbit 60
　Rabbit with beer and prunes 60
　Spicy honey glazed rabbit 60–61
Raita 38
Ratatouille 37, 114
Rice
　Rice pudding 126–7
　Risotto bianco *see* Risotto
　　Milanese
　Risotto con uova 116
　Risotto Milanese 115–16
　Turkey risotto 53
Roasting, general rules for 62–3
Root vegetable casserole 115

Sauces
　Apple sauce 118
　Barbecue sauce (1) 80
　Barbecue sauce (2) 103–4
　Bolognese sauce 104
　Caramel sauce 123–4
　Chicken liver and lemon sauce
　　40–41
　Chilli sauce 104–5
　Cranberry sauce 105
　Creole sauce 105
　Curry sauce 38
　Dál sauce 16
　Espagnole or Spanish sauce 106
　Fish sauce 30

Fruit syrup 124
Gooseberry sauce 47
Honeyed apricot sauce 46–7
Marsala wine sauce 48
Pineapple sauce 49–50
Plum sauce 106
Polish sauce 102
Port sauce 50
Sweet-sour sauce 107
Tarragon sauce 41
Vinaigrette sauce 68
and see Fondues
Sauerbraten 75
Shortcrust pastry 71–2
Slow-cooking method, the 7–8
Smoked haddock Savoy 24–5
Sole, baked 29–30
Soup-making, general rules for
    11–12
Soups and soup-stews
  Beef goulash soup with dumplings 14
  Chicken and prawn gumbo 17–18
  Cock-a-leekie soup 14–15
  Cream of corn soup 15–16
  Creole soup 20
  Curry soup 18
  Dál soup 16
  Fish chowder 16–17
  Oatmeal soup 19
  Oatmeal and leek soup 19
  Philadelphia pepperpot (or
    Pepperpot soup) 19–20
  Split pea or lentil soup 18
  Scotch (or Barley) broth 20
Spiced fish, casserole of 21–2
Sponge mixture 120
Stock 12–13, 67
Stracotto 76
Stuffing 58, 78, 89
Sweet dishes
  Apple butter 118
  Apple Charlotte 119
  Apple crunch 119
  Apricot upside-down cake 120
  Baked apples 117–18
  Baked custard 123
  Caramel custard (Crème caramel)
    123

  Chocolate fondue 121–2
  Danish apple cake 119
  Hot fruit salad 124
  Macaroon pear crunch 126
  Orange custards with caramel
    sauce 123–4
  Pears Alma 126
  Pears Hélène 126
  Pears in wine 125–6
  Poached fruit 124
  Prunes in cider 125
  and see Puddings

Tea breads and cakes
  Banana bread 130
  Boston brown bread 130–31
  Bran bread 131
  Carrot cake 131–2
  Fruit cake 132
  Honey cake 132
  Indian bread 131
Temperature settings 7–9
Tian 114
Tongue, directions for cooking 94,
    101–2
Tripe Lyonnaise 102–3
Trout 29–30
Tuna fish loaf 30–31
Turkey
  Stuffed turkey breasts 51–2
  Turkey casserole 52
  Turkey risotto 53
  Turkey terrine 54
  Turkey with cherries 52–3
  Turkey with cranberries and
    honey 53
  Turkey with Marsala wine 53

Veal
  Braised veal Catalane 96–7
  Fricandeau of veal 97
  Galantine of veal 97–8
  Osso buco 98
Venison 61

White fish, baked 22–3

Patricia Jacobs
The Best Bread Book   70p

Everything you need to know to bake delicious loaves, rolls and buns . . .
Easy to follow and attractively illustrated, these recipes for more than
fifty different breads are graded from 'easy' to 'experienced bakers only'.
Crammed with hints and guidance.

Michel Guérard's Cuisine Minceur   £1.50

'An entirely new cuisine – elegant cookery without butter, cream, flour –
built on classic principles without the classic calories. The dishes are as
spectacular as they are delectable' PUBLISHERS WEEKLY

'A delight. The approach is fresh, very professional and full of intriguing
ideas . . . provides new hope for all those who wish to keep their youth,
looks and health and still go on enjoying their food'
FINANCIAL TIMES

Theodora FitzGibbon
A Taste of Paris   £1.75

'Every food lover, every Paris lover, should buy this. The photographs
have been skilfully chosen and are most evocative . . . La Mère Catherine in
the Place du Tertre, the original Tour d'Argent, the late lamented Les
Halles . . . pure nostalgia' GUARDIAN

'No cookery reference shelf would be complete without a collection of
the books of that great cook Theodora FitzGibbon . . . dishes from French
cookery that even the most humble of cooks can produce with ease . . .'
SUNDAY TELEGRAPH

You can buy these and other Pan Books from booksellers and
newsagents; or direct from the following address:
Pan Books, Sales Office, Cavaye Place, London SW10 9PG
Send purchase price plus 20p for the first book and 10p for
each additional book, to allow for postage and packing
Prices quoted are applicable in the UK